The Fifth Dimension
New Beginnings

Messages from Jesus
Joan Wallace

BALBOA.
PRESS
A DIVISION OF HAY HOUSE

Balboa Press books may be ordered through booksellers or by contacting:

Balboa Press
A Division of Hay House
1663 Liberty Drive
Bloomington, IN 47403
www.balboapress.com
1-(877) 407-4847

Because of the dynamic nature of the Internet, any web addresses or links contained in this book may have changed since publication and may no longer be valid. The views expressed in this work are solely those of the author and do not necessarily reflect the views of the publisher, and the publisher hereby disclaims any responsibility for them.

The author of this book does not dispense medical advice or prescribe the use of any technique as a form of treatment for physical, emotional, or medical problems without the advice of a physician, either directly or indirectly. The intent of the author is only to offer information of a general nature to help you in your quest for emotional and spiritual well-being. In the event you use any of the information in this book for yourself, which is your constitutional right, the author and the publisher assume no responsibility for your actions.

Any people depicted in stock imagery provided by Thinkstock are models, and such images are being used for illustrative purposes only.
Certain stock imagery © Thinkstock.

Printed in the United States of America.

ISBN: 978-1-4525-7484-4 (sc)
ISBN: 978-1-4525-7486-8 (hc)
ISBN: 978-1-4525-7485-1 (e)

Library of Congress Control Number: 2013909297

Balboa Press rev. date: 06/07/2013

This book is dedicated to my family. Thank you, Richard, Dawn, Joey, Serena, and Leona, for your love and continued acceptance of my becoming who I am, and for knowing that it is but a speck of time within our infinite connectedness.

Table of Contents

Acknowledgments

It is a sincere pleasure to thank all those who have participated in my ever-expanding enlightenment process. Many have helped bring me to the place where I could hear Jesus's messages. I thank Jesus for his continued patience and love as I worked through the issues in my life and cleared blocks that kept me from writing for short periods of time. It truly was a process and an ebb and flow in and out of my connectedness with Oneness. Hearing his salutation of "My Precious One" as we connected each day that I wrote was amazing and so full of love. His embraces when I needed them filled me with amazing joy and brought me to the place of truly experiencing Oneness.

During my first personal encounter with Jesus several years ago, I was told to seek out the Unity Church of Nashville. "They will help you heal," He said. It took me a couple of months to do so, and the first person I met there was Gene Skaggs, who was teaching a class on *A Course in Miracles* that day. From his first hug of welcome, we have become fast friends. I had read *A Course in Miracles* a couple of years earlier, and Gene worked with me to help clear my blocks to living the principles of *A Course in Miracles* and writing this book. It has been an enlightening process for me, and I am now teaching these principles to others.

I would like to thank both Gene and Anderson Skaggs for trusting me to edit their book, *Anderson Speaks Again: Ushering in a New World*, which I volunteered to do through Divine prodding. It was through editing this book, with Anderson as my guide, that I was able to learn about the coming paradigm shifts and new world order. Once the book was completed, and I was filled with a great sense of accomplishment, I was finally able to acknowledge the Divine nudges I had been receiving for years to write my own book. This book begins where Anderson's book ends.

I would also like to thank those who have taken the leap of faith with me toward building our City of Light. It is in the early planning phase as I write this book and was the initial purpose for the book. Our City of Light will be a fully self-sustainable community practicing living in Oneness. We will use the principles set down in this book and the next as our guiding light as we move more and more into learning how to *be* in Oneness. As Jesus explained to me multiple times while writing this book, "It is all a process of experiences, each one building upon the last, and expanding who We are as children of God."

Introduction

As I sit in my home office writing this introduction, I have paused to reflect on my life. In looking back, I can clearly see a very strong pattern of divine intervention and assistance that has guided me since my early childhood. From my near-death experience at age two to my narrating this book, I have been blessed to receive Divine messages, wonderful ideas, and solutions to the problems I have encountered throughout the different phases of my life. Throughout my life, I have always been spiritual. Even as a child, I volunteered to teach religious classes at my church. I have been actively involved in spiritual teaching and counseling in one way or another, my whole life.

As I walk my path, I am learning to *be* and to accept the now that presents itself to me in each moment. This has been quite a challenge for me at times, as I am a consummate planner. My many years of experience in IT program and project management have led me to plan, plan, and plan some more, and now I am in the midst of leaving that phase of my life behind.

I am as excited as a child is at Christmas as I await the new opportunities that will present themselves to me at just the right timing. When I write, I look forward to being draped in the peacefulness that surrounds me as I connect with Jesus, and then I smile and listen for the words to come to me.

Near-Death Experience

My near death-experience when I was two was very profound and opened me up to a world in which most people are completely unaware. I sustained a severe blow to the head and crumpled to the floor in a heap. Before losing consciousness, I remember thinking I was going to die. What occurred next shocked me. All of a sudden, I was looking down at myself from the corner of the room. I could see my mother run into the room and scoop me up. At that point, I began to move away from the room, our house, and then the planet. I saw stars and planets everywhere around me, and then I was flying through them so fast that I couldn't discern them any longer. The next thing I remember was being held and hugged by a beautiful angel. She gently held me close, and I felt so much love and joy that I thought I might burst.

The next memory I have is of walking with the angel hand in hand on a path through beautiful countryside. There was a lake on the left and a bench on the right side. I saw lots of trees, flowers, birds, butterflies, and baby animals. There was a sweet fragrance of flowers in the air. I felt true peace and a strong sense that I belonged there.

Then the angel picked me up and sat on the bench with me on her lap. She told me she had something very important to say to me. She said, "You're not supposed to be up in heaven at this time. You're supposed to be back with your family." She raised her hand, swept it across the horizon, and showed me my family as she asked, "Don't you want to go home to your family?" I loved being up in heaven, so I shook my head and said, "No!" I began to cry while thinking I might have to go back, and she gently held me close while she rocked and reassured me.

The angel tried several more times to persuade me to go back to my family. All of them failed, until she showed me what life was going to be like for my twin brother without me. When she showed him to me from this new perspective, I remembered that we had agreed to come down together and that our life purposes were very closely intertwined. The angel told me he would be lost without my help. The angel again asked, "Would you like to go back to your family now?" As soon as I nodded my head yes, I was whisked back into my body at the hospital. Apparently, while I was deciding whether to come back, I had been in a coma for two weeks and had showed no signs of awakening.

Once back at the hospital, it was very dark, and I didn't recognize anything. I didn't know where I was. I was scared because there was no one around and nothing looked familiar. I slowly climbed out of bed, walked to the door, and looked out. The left end of the long hallway was dark with dim lights over doorways. At the other end, I saw a desk with a dim light and a person sitting there. With trepidation, I slowly began to walk toward the light. Once I was within ten feet of the counter, the nurse saw me, jumped up, and yelled, "Get back to your bed, young lady, or I'm going to spank you!"

I turned around to run back to where I came from, but all I could see were identical doorways. I didn't recognize which doorway I had come through; they all looked the same. I ran from door to door and looked inside until I found an empty bed with the blankets pulled back. It took me several tries to get back up into the bed, as it was much too tall for me. Once there, I covered myself completely with the blankets and hoped she wouldn't come find me. I was really scared and asked myself, "Where am I? Where is my family?"

I fell asleep almost immediately and awakened the next morning to see my mother smiling down at me with tears in her eyes. She scooped me up and hugged me, and although it felt good, it also seemed like she would never let go. I was so happy to see her. She stayed with me through that day and the next. At the beginning of the third day, after the doctor visited and gave his permission, I was allowed to go home to my family.

I remember that I couldn't wait to see my brother. The first thing I remember is running up and hugging him. I felt a bond that was stronger than ever. I decided at the moment that I would take care of him for the rest of his life. I don't have any other specific memories of what life was like upon my return home. It seems I just inserted myself back into my family at the point where I had left off.

I Don't Know. I Just Know.

From early childhood on, I can't tell you how many times I have given answers to questions, usually overheard and not asked of me directly. I would answer the question and then hear them respond with, "How did you know that?" My response was always, "I don't know. I just know." I also didn't keep count of the number of times that I had my IQ tested. It seemed that every time I went to a new school, I would be asked to go to the office to take an IQ test after a few months. I didn't know it at the time, but I was tapped into the Universal Divine Knowledge.

When I was in the third grade, I had a dream in which one of my school friends was sick and died. The next morning, I told my grandmother, who lived with us at the time, about my dream. She told me not to worry about it and that everything was fine. My girlfriend wasn't at school that day, and when I asked the teacher where she was, she told me she was sick. Two days later, the teacher announced in class that she had died of pneumonia the night before.

I was terror-stricken. I thought that my dream had caused her death. I went home and cried. My grandmother explained to me that certain people have a gift of knowing what is about to occur. She said she had the same gift and that when she was my age, she too had known a friend was going to die. She told me not to tell people because they might think that I was crazy. That made me even more scared. I didn't want to have a gift that would cause people to think I was crazy or that could possibly cause someone to die. My grandmother continued to reassure me that it was a gift, that I didn't cause it in any way, but part of me wasn't so sure.

In high school, two incidences of "knowing" come to mind. My freshman year, I awoke early one morning after seeing a vision of my father in a car accident. In my vision, I watched the whole thing in slow motion and saw that he was hurt very badly. I knew it wasn't a dream, so I jumped out of bed and ran to awaken my older sister. She told me I was dreaming and to go back to bed. I knew it was real, so I then awakened my older brother, who told me to go back to bed. I was crying by then. I went back to my sister and begged her to please get up and help me find him. When they continued to ignore me, I went back to bed and cried.

About an hour later, the phone rang, and my older brother answered it. It was the local hospital. My father had been broadsided in a terrible car accident and was in the emergency room. They didn't know if he was going to make it and wanted us to come down to the hospital as soon as possible, as he was asking for us. His back was broken as well as numerous ribs, and one of them had punctured his lung. My brother looked at me and asked me, "How did you know?" I answered, "I don't know. I just saw it all in my vision and knew it was real."

The second incident was when my twin brother was playing football in high school. During our sophomore year, he was playing a preseason game in a nearby city at precisely the same time I was doing the evening dishes at home. All of a sudden, I saw a vision of him at the football game, and that he had badly injured his arm. I walked out of the kitchen and told my dad he was hurt.

My dad asked how I knew, and I responded with my usual, "I don't know. I just do." Dad wasn't sure what to do so he got up and started pacing back and forth across our living room. After a couple of minutes, he sat down again, saying, "I guess I have to wait to find out since I don't know how to get ahold of anyone." About an hour later, my brother's coach called saying that he was at the hospital; he asked my dad to come down and pick up my brother. He had several deep lacerations to his arm that required more than 100 stitches to close the wounds.

Living with the Gift

As a younger adult, I didn't pay too much attention to my gifts. I had pushed them away because even my own family sometimes looked at me strangely. I saw the gifts as a good thing as well as a potential embarrassment. Since my brother's injury, I hadn't discussed my gifts with anyone, not even with my family or friends. There have been many events that have occurred similar to the ones below, but these are the ones that have stayed with me through the years.

I went through college knowing things that were way beyond the classes I was taking. I would frequently ask questions that the professors didn't know how to answer. After my sophomore year in college, I was offered a full scholarship to MIT to major in math or science. However, I turned it down because I knew that it wasn't what I wanted to do with my life. My professors and counselor thought I was crazy to turn the scholarship down, but I knew my life purpose was supposed to be about serving people. I just didn't have a sense of what that meant yet. I continued on and finished my degree in business with a minor is psychology.

Later, when I was thirty-four, married, and had become a stay-at-home mom with two young children, I had another significant event occur. I awoke in a panic early one morning after seeing a vision of my father dying. Every time I closed my eyes that day, I saw him die again. I was a nervous wreck by early afternoon and finally called my best friend to ask her to come and be with me. I tried calling Dad at least twenty times that day. On one of my calls my stepmom answered and told me, he wasn't home. I told her that she shouldn't leave him alone at all and that I was extremely worried about him. I asked her to please have him call me when he got home. (She didn't know of my gift, and I wanted to talk to Dad directly to make sure he understood the gravity of the situation.) I did not hear from him, and no one answered on my subsequent calls.

At around three o'clock the next morning our phone rang, and I answered with a knowing, "Dad's dead!" My older brother then asked me, "Who called you?" I answered, "No one. I just knew." Dad had died of a heart attack. I was devastated and felt that I hadn't done enough to try to save him. I felt I should have called more to try to reach him. I later learned from my angels that it was his time to go, and nothing that I could have done would have prevented his death. I was relieved to hear their message and was able to let go of the guilt I had been holding since his death. There have been many similar incidences, but these are the ones that seem to have affected me the most.

My Reawakening

In the summer of 2008, Dr. Chang, my neighbor and soon-to-be friend, took my hand the first time we met, and asked me, "Are you a healer?" Unbeknownst to him, this question sent me on a quest for its answer. It was in that quest for his answer that I was continuously guided by unseen Divine messages to learn what my purpose was for being here at this time.

In the years since, I have learned more about my other gifts of clairvoyance, clairaudience, clairsentience, and the other means of receiving Divine messages. This information led me to read many books on the subject. I also attended several seminars as I began to hear and learn more about the changes that were coming to our planet. Their messages all correlated with my visions, dreams, and the messages I was receiving. I can now answer Dr. Chang's question. Yes, I am a healer, as well as a messenger, medium, teacher, and leader.

In recent years, I have also been guided to read and study *A Course in Miracles* and the *Conversations with God* series, along with other Divine messenger books that I have had the pleasure to study. These books have expanded my spiritual knowledge and gifts. For the first time in my life I was able to clearly understand the gifts that I had been given and the purpose for their use. It was during this period that I began to clearly understand how the messages I had been receiving throughout my life had guided me in my search for truth.

At the beginning of 2012, I had the privilege of editing the book *Anderson Speaks Again: Ushering In a New World* by Gene Skaggs and found it to be both enlightening and profound. I had attended a weekly *Course in Miracles* study group that Gene was teaching, and he announced one evening that he had completed his new book channeled from Anderson. After the class, I was guided to speak to Gene and volunteered to edit his book. Little did I know that I would actively participate as a medium for Anderson during the entire editing process. I still communicate frequently with him to this day.

The morning after I agreed to edit the book, Anderson awoke me around 3:30 a.m. and asked me to go to my computer and write. He gave me instructions for what to do that day and let me know that he would be with me as I edited the book later that day. Subsequently he would awaken me early each morning and give me explicit instructions on what to do with my day. He was also with me whenever I edited the book. At that time, I was also working full-time as an IT consultant, so it felt very much like working two full-time jobs. However, I enjoyed each moment I spent with Anderson and learned a lot in the process. He is a beautiful soul with high energy, love, and a great sense of humor. It was truly an amazing experience.

Throughout this experience and my continued study, meditation, and prayer I have been guided to meet and mingle with many similar-minded souls. Together We have been nudged to begin a City of Light sustainable community for living in Oneness. We are excited to be a part of the new world paradigm shift. As Anderson has laughingly told me, "Strap on your seat belt and get ready for the ride of your life."

At the end of April 2012, I was guided to quit my IT consulting position so that I could devote my time to my spiritual advancement and planning our community of Oneness. It was not an easy decision, as I enjoyed helping others reach their corporate IT goals while making a comfortable living. Although my income has dropped to nearly zero now, I am thoroughly enjoying learning all that I am as a child of God. I have fully stepped into my purpose for being here. Throughout the writing process, Jesus has continued to remind me that all my needs will be provided for and with the highest and best outcome.

Writing This Book

This book has come to me in answer to my prayers for guidance on how to lead a community in Oneness. Our City of Light will come to fruition as a result of many years of spiritual growth and a want for a better future for our children and their children and their children, ad infinitum. Jesus has explained it to me this way:

> "The community will be an example for the entire world to witness the beauty, love, and joy of living in Oneness. You may choose to allow others to study your community so that they may learn from your example. You will also develop the knowledge and experience that may lead you to assist others in building similar communities around the world. You will not be alone in this endeavor, as We will send you many enlightened others to assist with your manifestation of your Oneness Community.
>
> As you grow spiritually, many gifts will be awakened in you and others that will help you bring your community into fruition. This community will be like none built for thousands of years on your planet. You cannot imagine what it will be like. You will enjoy the experience of participating in the new advancements in technologies that will be used for the design and creation of your community. The energy of all those who will participate will enhance the core power of living in Oneness."

I originally thought I would write one book with two parts. The first section was to cover spiritual concepts, and the second part was intended to give detailed instructions on how to build this community and live daily in Oneness. Now that the first part is complete, I have been guided by Jesus to publish the first section as a separate book; the second section will follow in another book. The book you are about to read will lay the foundation for the next book that I will immediately begin writing with Jesus once this one is complete. I hope that you find these messages to be a guiding light for you on your path. I know that I have.

"You have prayed for help in assisting you to learn how to live in Oneness, and this book is the answer to your prayers. In learning the answers to your questions, you will also be able to provide invaluable information for all on your planet. You will be provided advanced concepts, examples, and practical exercises to incorporate into your daily lives.

The world will need to be spoon-fed with incremental information that lays the groundwork for the next level of spiritual growth. This book describes where most of you are currently within your spiritual evolution, then provides contrasting examples of how advanced societies live in Oneness on other planets.

Moving from a third to a fourth, then a fifth-dimensional world creates many opportunities for spiritual growth for those who choose this path. Within these new dimensions, there will be many spiritual growth opportunities. Within these opportunities, you will also have a responsibility to ensure that you are living from love and your spirit self. The books I will give to you are meant as a guide so that you may understand all that is available to you and how to best use these gifts.

My next book I will write with you will be a guide for all those on your planet to learn how to actively live in Oneness. Within My *A Course in Miracles* book, there was much for all to learn about letting go of your egoic thought system. It was written to assist you in remembering who you are as children of God and to prepare you for living in a fifth-dimensional world. The next book and its workbook will be a guide on how to actually live your day-to-day lives in Oneness."

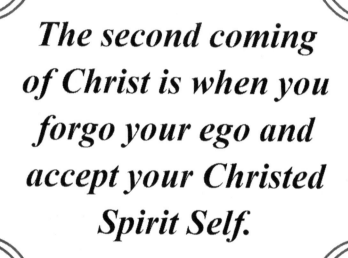

The second coming of Christ is when you forgo your ego and accept your Christed Spirit Self.

Chapter 1
The Purpose of this Book

Messages from Jesus

On Tuesday, May 14, 2012, I was awakened early in the morning with the request that I go to my computer to write my messages for the day. This seemed like a fairly typical day for me, as I was frequently awakened to receive messages. (If I didn't respond to the request right away, my cat would start howling or walk up and down on me until I awakened fully.)

These early-morning nudges to get up were always associated with a sense that whoever was trying to contact me was gently smiling and coaxing me out of bed. Therefore, I got up and sleepily walked to my laptop on our dining room table and logged in. I sat down, opened a new e-mail message, and typed the following:

> **Subject:** Messages: 05-14-12
> "Good Morning, My Precious One:
> This is Jesus and I am here to deliver information to you for your community. Today I ask you to write all day. If you are agreeable to that, I have much to say, and you are my chosen path for this information. Starting now, I'd like to dictate a book to you for you to use as a guide on your path for starting this community. You can do this and much, much more. If you are agreeable, then it is time to open your document and begin to write."

My first reaction to this message was complete shock. After having Jesus laughingly remind me to breathe several times, I inhaled deeply, opened a Word document, and began to type. What followed is this book, which Jesus has dictated to me over a seven-month period. I've placed the first message that followed from Jesus below:

> "I know that you are having a difficult time in grasping that I have chosen you to communicate through at this time. You

have some hesitation around this, and I want you to know that this is no mistake. You have prayed for guidance as you begin your Oneness Community, and I have come to you in answer to your prayers.

It is My hope that this book will assist you, your community, and your planet to open your hearts and minds to the possibility of a new way of *being* in your daily lives. These new possibilities are meant to be considered for adoption by all of the societies on your planet. While this may be a new way for you to consider living moving forward, it is not the only way. Most of the concepts you will hear from me are not new for your planet. Unfortunately, many have been discarded and long forgotten thousands of years ago. Now is the time for you to remember who you are and take your first step toward moving in the direction of how most advanced civilizations have lived on your planet in the past and how other spiritually advanced planets live at this time."

Early on in the book, I typed out the different chapters and subtitles I thought I wanted addressed in the book. Since that day, many of the chapters have changed significantly, as the information flowed from Jesus. I added new chapters and changed others to best serve Jesus's purpose of providing important concepts, universal laws, and information needed to understand living in Oneness.

The book was not written in order. Instead, I would browse all of the chapters and subheadings until I received the messages about which chapter or section Jesus wanted me to write that day. At other times I would be guided to just type the information I was given. I would later put this information into the appropriate section or a new chapter. Jesus and I added new paragraphs here and there to existing chapters, as I progressed through the book.

You will find that I have set off what Jesus was dictating to me so that you can easily identify what came directly from Him. As a new note, it turns out the remainder of the book is what Jesus has dictated to me, so all of it has been formatted differently. I have also capitalized pronouns used to describe Jesus (such as *I and My*) or Jesus along with ascended masters and other deities on the other side of the veil (for example, *We, Us, and Our*).

Being Selected to Write This Book

At the end of the first day of writing, I asked Jesus, "Why did you choose me to write this book?"

> You have been chosen for this endeavor because of your willingness to learn, listen, and most important, act. Many have listened but very few have wanted to act upon the information they were given. Your ability to understand and ask the right questions makes giving you this information easy for Us here on this side. It is your asking for Our help and wanting to do for your fellow beings that allows this to happen. Without the asking, We cannot assist.

> This planet is in need of many things. I will keep your messages to those that will assist you and others to learn to live in Oneness. Trust in yourself and know that We will assist you throughout the process, and all that you require will be provided to you. You will also be given the opportunity to learn how other planets live, and you will have the opportunity to write about them. You will see how more advanced societies live, work, and raise their children. Their lives are very simple, but they are much more advanced than your civilization. I will now tell you these words of wisdom: "Living simple lives allows for joy, peace, and harmony to abound." The belief systems of advanced societies are in alignment with the Universal Consciousness. They know who they are as part of the Universal Oneness, and this is ever-present in their consciousness. They don't have the challenges you have with your egoic thought system on Earth because of this knowing.

> There are many things that your planet does not currently understand about science and energy. We are working closely with many of your scientists to help them come to a more complete understanding of the universe and the properties under which it operates. Many in the scientific communities around the world have asked for guidance. We are available to guide them to new discoveries that will allow you to begin healing yourselves and your planet. We will describe in greater detail how your planet will appear in the fourth and fifth dimensions later in this book.

Your community will be a confluence of diverse beings wishing to co-create a community of Oneness. As time progresses, there will be new scientific discoveries that will manifest from your creative energy to complement your lives. Building and growing your community will not be an easy task. You will encounter many types of people with different personalities in various states of enlightenment. A few will wish to impose their beliefs onto you and change what you are doing. It will be important for you to remain a strong leader that guides your group to their full awakening. Much patience will be required. Remember that I will be there with you to assist you through these periods of discourse. Please remain patient with each of these beings, as they are coming from a place of fear or a feeling of lack and need your assistance in seeing themselves for who they really are.

You have much to learn about these new concepts, and you will need to continue to seek daily Divine guidance in all situations. Continue your work with enlightened others and teach these principles to others so that you can continue to be more within your spirit self. Working with others will also serve to heighten your gifts and hone them to their highest potential. Your prayers have been answered in that you now know it is time for you to step into your power and accept all that you can do. We are grateful you are open to the changes you need to make in order to show up as the leader you were intended to be. This book, your daily meditations, and working with other masters and archangels will assist you in developing the other gifts that are intended for you. Please know that you are following the correct path to your desired outcome.

Purpose of the Book

The purpose of this book is to provide the human race with the tools to begin a new shift in consciousness. This new shift is meant to create a new way of *being* human. The shift in the energy coming into your planet brings with it the potential for each person to move toward living in the Christ Consciousness of a fifth-dimensional world. With this new energy, you can now choose to become a planet of love and Oneness, which was intended for you since the beginning of your time.

Your Christian teachings tell you of a second coming of Christ, and I am here to tell you that this time is upon you now. However, it will not occur in the way some of you have fearfully believed. It will not be a judgment day. Nor will I physically appear on Earth at this time. It is however, a joyous time of awakening the Christed aspect within each of your souls. You see, the second coming of Christ is when you forgo your ego and begin to recognize your soul's place in God's Sonship. We have been holding your place for you, waiting for the time when you are ready to accept it as your own. For it is who you really are in Oneness.

In order to awaken the Christ consciousness within yourselves, you must turn inward to learn who you really are as children of God. Awakening your Christ consciousness begins with learning how to live your life with Love in every moment, just as I endeavored to live here on Earth thousands of years ago. This requires you to quiet your egoic thought system and *be* in the moments of *now* so that you can consciously choose to be the reflection of God's love toward everyone who appears in your life.

Living in Oneness requires humanity to shake off their current belief systems to embrace the truth of their existence. You are all children of God, part of the Christed Sonship. Oneness is the state of manifesting physically, as in a human body, while remaining in constant connection with the Universal Divine Consciousness. Before you are incarnated on Earth, you are each part of the Universal Divine Consciousness as spirits/souls. This book teaches you the truth of your existence and how life may begin anew for the human race. Use it as you move forward in your ascension in spirituality.

This book is also a continuation of My *A Course in Miracles* book written through Helen Schucman. It is meant to reinforce what you have learned from her book and add new information that the world was not yet ready to hear previously. The information is being sent to you in increments so that you can assimilate the information in a manner that will allow you to learn and adopt each aspect as it is made available to you.

Please do not attempt to skip reading, experiencing, and internalizing the information contained in *A Course in Miracles*, as that step in your spiritual growth cannot be circumvented. Even if you already know much of the material from other sources, you will still gain valuable insights into how your egoic thought system works and how to practice choosing wisely in your daily lives.

You must separate from your egoic thought system to truly *be* in Oneness. This is a difficult accomplishment even for those who have carefully studied *A Course in Miracles* and nearly impossible for those who haven't. You are on this planet for a purpose. It is up to you to determine if or when you will awaken to know your purpose. Do not fret that you are not at a place where you think you must be, for that is impossible. Each and every one of you are exactly where you are supposed to be at this moment, and if you are reading this book right now, then you should rejoice in the fact that you are awakening. There are also many who are not intended to awaken during this lifetime, and that is exactly where they are supposed to be.

This book is intended to show your planet the potential of living within this new way of *being*. Some of the concepts and examples of Oneness I will use in this book will cause many of you to step back and question your current beliefs, and I will say, "That's great!" as that is also part of its purpose. Others may not be able to fully adopt or understand what is written here, and I would say that it does not matter. Your planet requires this information to begin their lives anew in a manner that will bring them great peace, joy, and love. You are becoming your own internal teacher, and this information is here for you to use for that purpose.

Some of you may find that you have learned certain information contained in this book from other sources, and I would also say, "That's great. You are seeking spiritual knowledge from different sources, and this will serve you well." I would ask you to view this information as a review and reinforcement of what you have already learned. There are many other messengers who have been given similar information contained in this book. They too have been chosen to write this information in different ways so as to appeal to as many souls as possible. Each person must hear the information in the way that is best suited for him or her. The information contained in this book is meant to appeal to as many souls as possible, including Christians and all other religions.

I hope that you will be awakened by the messages contained in this book. If not, do not lament; there are many other genres in which to get this information that speaks to your soul. Continue to seek that which your soul desires to hear. Messages have always been and will continue to be sent to your planet so that you may know that you are not alone in your connectedness to God. We are only a thought away and will be happy to respond to your requests of help and information.

Beginning Anew

Your planet has been mired in egoic thoughts and false beliefs for thousands of years, and that has kept you from knowing who you really are for much of your human existence on this planet. Many times in your history, your civilizations have been brought to this place of spiritual awareness and Oneness. Unfortunately, none of these societies has prevailed in sustaining this way of *being* in Oneness. Perhaps the time is now? I would like to ask everyone who reads this book to please consider this as an invitation to be the ones who accomplish this sustainability now and on into infinity. Let us welcome Earth back into the fifth dimension together and move it forward to its rightful place in the Divine Sonship.

Consider this your new beginning, a time of rebirth. It is your opportunity to move beyond all of the drama, and made-up beliefs to a place of knowing and living within Oneness, peace, love, joy, harmony, and service to one another. It is through this peace, love, joy, harmony, and service to others that you will see God in everyone and everything, and that is the first step toward Oneness.

In order to move into Oneness you will need to discard the belief that you are separate from God.

Chapter 2
Your Human Existence

Understanding the Human Existence

During many periods in your history when your connectedness to the Universal Divine was lost, God sent you messengers and leaders to help bring you back to your self-awareness and Oneness. I was one of those special messengers. I have lived on your planet several times, and each time I brought messages of how to live in Oneness. During my period here on Earth, much was taught of Oneness and how to live a life of love, joy, and peace. My teachings and miracles were accepted by many but rejected by many at the time. It took my death before many realized that the messages given were worthy of consideration and should be adopted as a means of living.

There have also been many other masters who were sent to all areas and all races on your planet to assist in your learning who you are as a child of God and your role in Oneness. Most of these enlightened beings were not accepted while they walked the planet. Some were persecuted and others ignored. Those who have been remembered have had their life stories preserved and retold through thousands of years. Unfortunately, in the process, most of their teachings have been changed and little has been kept of their original content.

The rejection of Oneness is the nature of the egoic thought system. The ego operates out of its fear of the unknown and creates seemingly valid reasons not to embrace Oneness. For those who do not understand, their ego fears Oneness and from that fear creates the resistance to it. The fear is typically generated out of the thought that one is going to be punished for not living in Oneness or there will be a loss of personal identity or individuality. Nothing could be further from the truth. As you will soon experience, it is only through conscious living that you will find the love, peace, happiness, and joy in your life that you each so desperately crave. Some of you have already learned that if you are living from your egoic mind, then you will never find the elusive peace and love you seek. Please know that love, peace, and harmony are there for you at any time you choose to seek them out through your spirit self. You always have the option to choose to live through your spirit self in Oneness instead of your ego. Living in Oneness is where you can truly experience love, joy, peace, harmony, and happiness in your life.

The Evolutionary Process

In your history on Earth humans have had advanced capabilities far beyond what you can do today. Your world is three-dimensional today, and that has not always been the case. There have been numerous societies in your history that have lived at the fourth-, fifth-, and sixth-dimensional levels. Unfortunately, many shifted away from Oneness and lived from their egoic thought systems. Their thirst for power caused them to consider the catastrophic destruction of other societies using their advanced technologies. Through their ego they blocked their awareness of their connection in Oneness. They forgot who they were as children of God. They misused the gifts they were given in the fifth dimension. Because of their warring and self-destructive nature, they were stripped of their higher dimensional capabilities at that time, and Earth fell back into being a third-dimensional planet.

Your planet has once again grown in spiritual awareness to a point where many of you are ready to advance to the fourth and fifth dimensions. Earth is evolving as a planet and has begun to move from a third to a fifth frequencial planet. Learning to live in Oneness can be a lengthy process for some, as they must internalize what they will learn here and then apply it within their daily lives. There is much to accomplish to become ready to live in a fifth-dimensional world. We are here to assist you in all aspects of your ascension. As each of you has free will, you may want to remember that you must request assistance before it can be given to you.

In order to move toward Oneness, you will need to discard the belief that you are separate beings. It is in seeing everyone and everything that appears in your life as a part of you that allows you to begin to know Oneness. There is much for you to learn and practice to become a planet of Oneness within the fourth and fifth dimensions. The foundation and framework in which your world now operates must be set aside to support your new way of *being*. Many of you will soon begin to consciously step into your spiritual power to learn and understand the type of changes that need to occur. In your awakening process, many of you will be drawn to turn inward and connect to your spirit self to find what it is that you are seeking.

Your spiritual growth and process of change may occur rather quickly or not at all in this lifetime. Spiritual growth is always an individual process of expansion and contraction. It will occur at exactly the right timing for each person. People will choose the path that is right for them during their ascension process. All paths eventually lead to God. You are exactly where you are supposed to be, and all that is supposed to occur for you will happen in the right timing. Some will grasp the new concepts early and begin to live in Oneness relatively quickly, and some will not come to this realization for several lifetimes. Please love, accept, and support one another where ever you currently are, as you are exactly where you are supposed to be and do not require intervention from anyone. Each person is living out their experience in the way that is right for them.

Understanding the Egoic Thought System:

The egoic thought system seeks to enhance itself by external approval, external possessions, and external love. In contrast, the spirit self needs nothing. It is forever complete, safe, loved, and loving.

The egoic thought system was created out of a lack of understanding of your world. When you arrived on this planet from the spiritual realm, most of you had no memory of your past lives or where you had come from. Some of you arrived here with a general sense or concept of Oneness, but most of you were not aware of your origin or the understanding of its nature.

Through the well-intended interactions of your families, religions, teachers, friends, and acquaintances, you have developed an intricate egoic thought system. Unfortunately, much of what it holds in its memories is false information, which it uses to explain what occurs around you. In your search for understanding, you have also learned to assume what other people are thinking and what motivates their actions. After accepting these assumptions as facts, you react to others in ways that are less than loving and have created much drama in your lives.

Many of you have also learned through your religions about a God who is wrathful and punishing. Many of you have not thought to question these assumptions or to look inside your spirit self for the true answers. There have been many fallacies within your beliefs that have been passed on from generation to generation.

Very few of you have learned who you really are. We lovingly ask you to no longer accept or propagate these beliefs, teachings, and practices that no longer serve you. Please consider taking the time to connect to your spirit selves to learn who you really are. Learn your purpose for being on Earth during this lifetime. In doing this work to reconnect to your spirit self, you will find greater peace, joy, love, and happiness, as these are the emotions attached to the God part within you. You will also find the truth that resonates in your hearts.

As you turn inward to learn the truth, you must first be aware that there are things that you don't know, and more importantly, that you don't know you don't know them. In the learning of what you don't know, you will gain much insight into the workings of the universe. In this place of learning and searching for the truth, you will find much peace and happiness. Learning the truth creates a joy and thirst for further learning. As you become a student of the truth, you will begin to find the peace and love that is your birthright. The realization of your truth and the clarity of how everything operates in the universe assist with removing the fears your egoic minds have created.

Be aware that in turning to your spirit self for the truth, your egoic thought system may attempt to keep you from what you seek. Some of you have given your egoic thought system so much power that it does not want to relinquish it to your spirit self. In the process of turning inward, be gentle with yourself and understand that your ego may bring up some fears within you as a part of this process. You will encounter fears of the unknown, as you are turning away from the familiar and embracing self-reflection and self-truth. As you begin this process, allow yourself the space to feel the fear that will come up, but continue to seek the knowledge of who you are and your purpose for being here. Give your fears to God to release them. These fears are not real and not truly a part of you.

There are many ways the ego works to keep you from the truth of its inner workings. The egoic thought system likes to be right. It attempts to relieve you of guilt and shame by transferring the responsibility for your actions onto others. Your ego may tell you, "If he/she hadn't done this to me, then I would not have reacted as I did." You can probably think of many such thoughts you have had in your past. In addition, many of you can truly point a finger and say that terrible things were done to you by others. And We would agree. However, it is important to realize that what another does to you is one hundred percent a reflection of them and not of you. Once you understand this, you can accept responsibility for all that you do, then choose a different reaction in response to their actions. Consider another choice that is coming from love and not your ego. You can choose to do nothing or retaliate or ask yourself what the most loving response could be and then choose that option.

In further understanding your ego, it is important to know that your thoughts, words, and actions are coming from either love or fear. Whenever your thoughts, words, or actions are loving, they are coming from your spirit self. If they are fearful, they are coming from your ego. Better put, no matter what a person thinks, says, or does, they are in reality either showing you love or crying out for love. When you can really understand that people are either showing you love or asking for love, then you will know that the only reaction that you can have in response is to act in the most loving way you can to them. This doesn't mean that you have to endure abuse or disrespect of any kind. It means that you can respond from a place of love, and acknowledge their feelings and beliefs. Then you can choose whatever path you wish to follow moving forward. You always have a choice. You can decide to lovingly tell someone that you choose differently from him or her and then act accordingly.

Recognizing Egoic Thoughts

You can recognize egoic thoughts by paying attention to whether your thoughts, words, or deeds are coming from a place of love or fear. If they are not coming from love, then you are thinking through your egoic thought system and not your spirit self. Recognizing your ego at work can be one of the most challenging aspects of personal growth as you seek your spiritual path and move toward Oneness. Egoic thoughts usually show up as stories you think or tell others about yourself, a situation, or another person. These thoughts typically occur as a means for you to understand and/or explain what occurred. They are made up by your egoic thought system to help you look good to either yourself or others or both. All attempts to make yourself look good to yourself or to others originate from your egoic mind. These attempts can show up as stories or ways in which you believe you must dress, and/or act, and/or in what you think you should say around others. These thoughts or stories may also be attempts to feel socially accepted, or they can be used as a means of manipulation.

There are those who put others down or complain about others so that they can feel better about themselves. This is very prevalent in your schools, because so many are insecure in their self-awareness and put others down as a means of feeling better about themselves. These types of thoughts, words, and actions create the drama and negative emotions that have led to recent school shootings. Please understand that the cruelty that many perpetrate onto others will come back to them as negative karma until they learn from it. Once they begin treating others in a loving way and learn from their past, this completes the karmic experience.

These types of karmic experiences can complete in several ways. They may experience others treating them in similar, cruel ways so that they learn how it feels. At that point, they may recognize their actions were not loving and then choose to heal the situation by showing up more lovingly towards others. They may also turn to the Holy Spirit and ask Him to show them what they were supposed to learn from the experience and in the knowing and acting lovingly, they are released from the karma.

Once they have recognized that the situation was created out of the negative karma from their past transgressions, they can learn from and forgive all those involved. The negative karma releases when this type of behavior ceases in their lives. If their behavior continues, they will find that these negative karmic events continue to play out as the drama persists in their lives. The good news is that when you live your daily life from love, then the laws of negative karma have no effect on you.

Another means for determining if you are coming from your egoic thoughts or your loving spirit self is to step back and ask yourself how you feel about what has occurred. Do you feel joyful and loving about yourself, the others involved, and the situation in question? If your answer is yes, then you were most likely living from your loving spirit self and not your ego. But if you don't feel joy or love or you have negative feelings about the situation or person, then your actions came from your ego. Let your feelings guide you and your thought processes. Pay close attention to your emotions: they can be a very accurate gauge for how you have been living your life.

Please understand that there is nothing wrong with living through your ego, and that this is not an attempt to make you feel bad or less than in any way. It is important that you understand that the egoic thought system produces fear and feelings of lack in your perception of your world, and it is these thoughts that keep you from experiencing unconditional love and Oneness. We lovingly tell you this information so that you can be aware of how the ego operates and the consequences of staying under its control. When you recognize your ego at work, you can make a conscious choice to reset your thoughts and begin living from your spirit self once again.

Through understanding the egoic thought system, you will begin to recognize the shackles your egoic thoughts have placed on you and others. You will realize that these egoic thoughts are coming from your false beliefs about how the world operates. While you do this work, you will also begin to understand how your egoic thoughts have kept you from having the love and peace in your life that you so desperately seek. If you can truly understand this about your egos, then you can mindfully shift in consciousness to begin living in Oneness.

Releasing Egoic Thoughts

Releasing your egoic thought system is a process. While working to quiet your egoic thought system, you will find that it is a process of observation, recognition, and then choosing again. A miracle can occur at any instant that you are ready for it. It happens at that moment where you connect the dots and realize you have transcended your egoic mind and live purposefully with a loving intent for all those in your life . It requires a desire for change and the pursuit of a life lived from love. There is no greater joy than to love and be loved. Love is the driving force for all of humanity, no matter your origin of country, culture, or religious beliefs.

Be Mindful. Observation is the first step in moving away from the egoic thought system. It is a key ingredient to your success. Without the self-observation and review, one cannot recognize the origin of one's thoughts, words, or actions. This will take daily practice. Remember to take the time to observe and review your day and ask yourself the following questions:

1. **Observation:** How did I show up in my interactions today? Was I loving in my approach and intent to all those involved?

2. **Recognition:** Did I show up and act in the most loving way possible in each interaction? How do I feel about my role in each interaction?

3. **Choosing Again:** For those interactions that need correction, ask yourself, What could I have done differently that would have made the interaction one where all parties felt safe, loved, respected, and understood and still have attained a mutually desirable outcome?

4. **Allow the Holy Spirit to Assist You:** From now on, before you engage another, ask the Holy Spirit to speak through you. He will provide an interaction for you that will allow for the highest and best outcome for everyone involved.

This process will get easier over time as you practice living from your spirit self. Once you recognize your role in each interaction and determine how you could have shown up, you can begin to practice your new way of being. It will be a trial-and-error process as you recognize what works and what doesn't and their reactions to you. Obtaining the input of others so that you can learn how they perceived the event is also a good learning tool. It is best when the one you are asking also understands and recognizes when the ego is at work.

The most important thing to remember is to continue to move in the direction of *being* love in all your actions. Be gentle with yourself as you flow in and out of your egoic thought system. It is important for you to realize that each person who comes into contact with you will most likely be in a different place in their spiritual evolution and may not know of Oneness. These are the ones who have not awakened yet and may require more love, patience, and understanding as you work through your relationship with them.

After reading this section, some of you will immediately forget and go back to living through your egoic thought systems without beginning your observation of self. Understand that you may require frequent reminders of how you are living and that in every moment you have the option to choose again. If you continue to experience egoic challenges, perhaps you may consider studying *A Course in Miracles*. It was written to help you understand the ego and remember how you should be living each day. The workbook includes exercises that provide daily opportunities to practice being aware of your egoic thoughts. It presents you with opportunities to choose loving thoughts, words, and actions that emanate from your spirit self.

Practicing Living Through Love

As you practice living from love each day, you will begin to see egoic thoughts in others and realize that not so long ago, this was how you showed up to others. You can use daily experiences to practice living through love with those who are not aware. Be kind and gentle to them, as they are unaware and where you once were. For those who learn through observation, you can now provide them the opportunity to see you living from love.

It is also helpful in your learning process to help others observe, recognize, and choose again. Please be mindful that you not intrude in their experience. Obtain permission before offering assistance to help them look at their problems in a different light. If they grant their approval, then help them in the way in which they would like assistance. Remember to step aside and let the Holy Spirit speak through you. Keep in mind the saying, "When the student is ready, the teacher will appear." Also, know that, "As you teach, so shall you learn." Teaching others allows you to re-experience learning the information again and again. It reinforces your new beliefs and helps you internalize the concepts more fully. When you come from love, others will show up to you because they too want to remember who they are as children of God.

It would also be helpful for you to surround yourself with others who are living their lives coming from love. This is another means of reinforcing your new way of being. If you are continually exposed to others who are living from their egoic thought system, their behaviors and negative energy may drag you back down into living continuously in your egoic thoughts. It is easy to slip back into living through your ego when all who are around you are also living that way. You may want to consider making new friends with those who are seeking Oneness too and living from love. Having friends who are on a similar path provides each of you the mutual benefit of supporting each other throughout the process.

As you observe your new way of interacting and how you feel about them afterward, you will begin to feel a shift in your consciousness. Your moods will be elevated to one of joy and happiness. You will feel further connected to others and the Divine and feel like dancing in the wind. Living from love is who you really are and is your true purpose for being here. Enjoy the process as well as the results in each moment and know that you are exactly where you are meant to be. Understand this and see your brothers and sisters in the same light. Love and forgive them their transgressions as you forgive yourself. Love sent out to others not only goes to those you intend, but continues on to elevate others as well.

Your beliefs from the past have kept your planet in the past. It is now time to throw off these limiting beliefs and accept the inheritance that was intended for you since the beginning of your time.

Chapter 3
Three-Dimensional Belief Systems

Preparing for Ascension

Your planet is ascending from a third- to fourth-, then a
fifth-dimensional planet. In addition, all who are on your
planet now are ascending spiritually as well. In order for
you to ascend, you will need to understand the principles of
ascension and what benefits you may obtain as part of the
ascension process. During this ascension period, which has
not occurred on your planet for hundreds of thousands of
years, you have the opportunity to advance spiritually in what
could have taken you many, many lifetimes.

The ascension process is Divinely structured. It takes place
through raising the energy of your planet to higher frequency
ranges. This occurs gradually through the mass corona
solar plasma ejections, which are absorbed by Earth. These
energies are dispersed around Earth through the subterranean
crystalline grids. This wonderful ascension energy will be felt
by everyone. It will be the catalyst of change and ascension
for your planet. You will learn more about this energy in later
chapters.

To prepare for your ascension, you will need to understand
the truth of who you are within the Divine Universe. This
book is intended to explain what is occurring, the changes
that will expedite the process, and any misconceptions about
God that could hold you back. This chapter is intended to help
you come to know the truth of your Divine existence and your
interrelatedness to all that is in the universe. I would gently
ask that you now consider this time period as a turning point,
where Earth no longer considers itself disconnected from God
and remembers the truth of its existence.

To understand where your erroneous beliefs have come from, I will explain how they occurred. In your history, We have sent many messengers to help your planet understand its existence and how to live in Oneness. These messengers provided the information to their listeners in a pure form. But through the retelling, insertions, misunderstandings, and misrepresentations, vast misinformation has occurred over thousands of years. The messages have changed again and again, losing much of their purity along the way. Most of the changes to the original messages were made unintentionally. They came from forgetfulness or the inability to understand the previous teachings. Other misinformation was inserted to allow certain individuals to control the masses and gain power over them. I do not judge these practices but want you to understand their origin so that you may understand the truth.

It is also important to note here that these messages were given to people thousands of years ago. Most of these teachings were told in a way that the people in that period of history could best understand. Many of these teachings were parables and were never intended to become laws or to be carried forward through thousands of years. Although some of them are still appropriate examples in how to *be* today, they were intended only for those people during that period in history. This book is being written for you in the same manner so that you may understand within your own context. These are the messages intended for now and your immediate future and will be given to you incrementally because you can accept only so much at any given time. More messages will be forthcoming, and they will be progressive in nature. Please do not make them into more than they are. The new information will be intended for those who are on Earth at that time. It will relate to what is occurring at that time, and will assist them in moving further in their spiritual evolution process.

History of Belief Systems

Since man has appeared on Earth, he has created belief systems in order to understand the world around him. During

most periods of your history, when infants were born into
this world they had forgotten their origin and Oneness,
and because of this, they couldn't comprehend what it was
they saw around them. To give meaning to what they saw,
they believed the stories they were taught about people,
places, events, and things that helped them bring order and
understanding to what they experienced. Most of these
egoic teaching were innocently created. Unfortunately, most
of these teachings created beliefs that were false, but they
allowed people during these different times and places to
operate in what they perceived as a less fearful state within
their surroundings. No one is to be made wrong here. These
are merely the facts of your history.

In reality, these false beliefs have been perpetuated and
carried forward for a much longer time than suited any of
the generations that followed their origin. But because you
were lovingly taught by your parents, who were taught by
their parents, who were taught by their parents, and on and
on back through history, you believed them. Most generations
did not question them or consider that these beliefs might be
erroneous. They just accepted them as fact and obliviously
went upon their merry way.

Originally, man had the ability to remember who he was as
a child of God and his connectedness to all in the Universe.
But because of major negative events in your history, you fell
from being a fifth- to a third-dimensional planet, and those
abilities were suppressed and eventually forgotten. At other
times in your history, humans remembered who they are and
were able to live and communicate in Oneness, but through
a confluence of egoic choices and lack of spiritual teachings,
forgetfulness once again descended upon your planet.

Your lost societies of Atlantes, LeMuria, and Rama-Mu were
highly evolved societies of Oneness. Other smaller advanced
societies were formed in China, Egypt, Europe, and North
and South America. During these periods of knowing,
humans were able to communicate telepathically, and the
veil between the spiritual and Earth planes was lifted. They
understood their Oneness and lived simple lives of love,
contentment, peace, and harmony. They communicated with

those on the other side of the veil with ease and received guidance in their daily lives. Unfortunately, these societies were lost during times of disconnection with the Divine when Earth was at the farthest point in its circumnavigation within your galaxy.

You are at the beginning of another period of remembering on Earth as you begin your ascension process. This book is intended to educate you on what you are about to experience and how best to move up the rung into your next cycle of evolution. It is meant to be a GUIDE to assist you in creating a more advanced society where peace can descend upon your planet for thousands of years. As always, it is all a matter of choice. Each person must choose whether they want to move toward living as a more advanced society or not. If you are interested in learning about living within an advanced spiritual society, then this book is intended for you."

Current Limiting Beliefs

Your beliefs from the past have kept your planet in the past. It is time to throw off these limiting beliefs and accept the inheritance that was intended for you since the beginning of your time. It doesn't require much from you—a mere shift in your openness to believe differently from how you have been taught up to now. It requires you to understand that there are things you do not know, and understand that you don't know that you don't know them. And in the learning of them, your lives will be transformed in amazing ways. It does not require you to give up your beliefs in God, Buddha, Allah, Jesus, or any other gods you currently worship. Nor are you required to give up your religions. But, perhaps as an outcome of what you read in this book, you may wish to discard certain erroneous interpretations of your scriptures and holy books. You will know you are on the right path when you no longer have expectations of others and the paths they choose.

It is my hope that you will see how the limiting beliefs contained within your holy books have caused so much pain and sadness to their followers, and that this was never truly intended for you. You are not asked to discard all of your beliefs, only those that are incorrect and have never served you. The limiting beliefs that are keeping you from having a loving relationship with yourselves and all those in your lives are listed below:

1. That you are separate and individual beings and disconnected from God.

2. That God could possess anything but love for you.

3. That you are bad, have sinned, or have an original sin.

4. That you must do something to earn God's love.

5. That you must do something to earn God's forgiveness.

6. That you are inherently evil in nature and require control.

Contrary to what many of you have been taught, none of the above beliefs are true, nor did God at any time communicate these beliefs to anyone. Although they may appear in your holy books, they have come from erroneous retelling or the needs of previous generations to reinterpret the original messages or to control the masses at those times in history. Some of the individuals who changed the original messages throughout history used these changed "beliefs" to their advantage. Others made changes in the retelling through forgetfulness or as a means of trying to explain what they believed to be true about God. I do not judge these unintended beliefs or the reasons they came into being. I am merely saying that they are not true, that they no longer serve you, and that they should be set aside to make way for the truth. Your planet has now matured once again to a higher level of understanding that can allow you to shake off these false shackles and live your lives with a true knowing of your origin and who you really are.

Unfortunately, many on your planet will be unable to embrace these changes at this time and will choose to ignore them. There is nothing wrong in this choice either. They are where they are supposed to be in their spiritual path and are always in a state of grace no matter what their belief. Please be kind, understanding, and gentle with them, as they are where you once were, either earlier in this life or many lives ago. They are on their path of chosen experience, and all is how it is intended. They are you at their core and require nothing from you other than love, compassion, and understanding.

I will now take each of these beliefs and explain the limits they impose upon you. Then I will provide you with a replacement truth to know and understand that will allow you to expand your awareness of your Oneness. These are some of the things you don't know, and knowing and understanding them will bring about amazing and wonderful changes to your lives.

Erroneous Belief 1:
You Are a Separate Individual and Apart from God

In the beginning, there was only God. From the energy that is God, He created the Universe. All that is in the Universe is still God, but has expanded. A certain amount of this energy that is God has become planets, moons, stars, and all other particles in the Universe. Some of this energy has formed water, elements, plants, and physical beings on various planets. All of this is still a part of God and made from God's energy.

This is perhaps one of the most challenging understandings of truth that many of you may have a difficult time accepting. You were taught from your earliest time of understanding that you are separate from one another, and now I am telling you that is not your truth. Although you appear to be separate and apart from another body on your planet, you are in fact, all made up entirely of God's energy force. Every cell, molecule, atom, and subatomic particle you have labeled in your world as something else is, in truth, God. As God's energy, you are all connected. As such you have retained certain inherently Divine qualities that you are currently unaware are available to you. There is nothing you need to do to remain connected, for in truth, it is impossible to disconnect. We will discuss these qualities in other chapters of this book.

This one simple concept is the core to all other beliefs about God. From this fact, you can gain understanding of all the

26

other truths about yourself, the universe, and God. Within this concept, you will find the knowledge of the universe and grow to understand all of your connectedness within the All that is God. Each and every one of you is truly a child of God and a part of the Sonship. Everything is connected to everything else in the universe, and what one does to another ultimately becomes what one has done to itself. We are all a part of God, and God is a part of us. Each of us is connected to one another and to everything else on our planet and to everything within the universe. There is no separation from the All That Is. Our energy goes out from us and intermingles with everything around us.

Erroneous Belief 2:
That God Could Possess Anything but Love for You

There are so many beliefs in all of your religions that speak of a wrathful and judgmental God. In truth, God is pure love and as such cannot be anything other than love.

God's love does not judge; His love only honors.

> God's love does not punish; His love embraces.
> God's love does not require anything from you.
> His love merely wishes you to be joyous, happy, and
> peaceful in your experience within the here and now.

It really is that simple. God is Love and God can only be Love. As you are part of God at your core, you are also Love. In your Earthly experience, you have merely forgotten this truth and act out in incongruence with your love. In awakening your soul and remembering, you will move back to your truth of love and act accordingly. It will take practice on your part, as you have manifested your egoic thought system to explain what you have not up until now known or understood about yourself. Your egos have made up vast "stories" about yourselves, your history, others, and your world in an attempt to understand what it sees. As I have mentioned previously, these stories have been passed from generation to generation in a perpetuation of many untruths. In the past, loving and caring parents and teachers have taught you erroneous information for generations, but now it is time for you to know the truth. It is the egoic mind that creates the complexities of having to explain all that it does not understand. Know that unconditional love is very simple. Love everyone and everything equally, without reservation or conditions.

In this special period of time, We ask you to open your eyes, minds, and hearts to fully understand who you really are so that you may *be* in your true spirit self. Seek out the masters, teachers, messengers, and healers We have sent to help you understand these concepts and your purpose for being here. The author of this book is one of them. These enlightened ones will assist you in understanding in more detail all that is available to you and how to incorporate these new beliefs into your daily lives. Knowledge, purpose, and practice are your stepping-stones back onto the path toward Oneness and ascension.

Erroneous Belief 3:
You Are Bad or Have an Original Sin

Each child born into your world is pure Love. They do not possess sin or carry sin with them from anyone or anything. You need merely look upon a newborn child to see the innocence and love. In your own naiveté and innocence, you have taught your children they are separate, and that life is harsh, difficult, and evil. It is time to set aside these false beliefs and embrace the truths you have yet to hear. Know that you cannot do anything that will keep you from God's love or heaven.

Your current beliefs and social structures of life were all created from a lack of understanding of your origin. There is no one to be made wrong here. If your ancestors had known and understood their origin, they would have chosen another way, and your world would look different now. Many of you are just now learning these truths, and We are excited to see that you have sought to read this book. Please read these truths and assimilate them, as they will guide you toward your purpose and a life of love and happiness.

This book is intended to show you what options you haven't known to consider until now. Where your societies are at right now is derived from the outcome of all the collective choices made on your planet throughout your history. These decisions have played out in a manner that has led to a state of vast unknowing at this time. It is sad for us to see you feel so badly about yourselves. We know that you are sinless, and will be forever. Some of you have merely chosen to experience your human life in a way that is opposite of that from which you were created. In truth, each of you is pure Love at your core spirit self and are incapable of anything but love.

Some of you have chosen to live as love and others have not. Those who live as love do so from their spirit selves, and those who live from their egos live from fear. This is another of the more complex concepts that many have been unable to grasp and understand. You are here as a life force of God to experience all that is available to you in the here and now. You have a choice in each moment of every day to experience your life from your egoic perspective or from your spirit self. The decision to live from love is always there for you to make at any point in time. A mere shift in perspective can lead you to love and truth.

Erroneous Belief 4:
You Must Do Something to Earn God's Love

This erroneous belief comes from religious teachings and social beliefs. It is another belief that We would ask you to consider setting aside. The fact is that you need do nothing to earn God's love, for it is yours always, as it was in your past, is now, and continues into infinity. To have to earn God's love would support the false assumption that you are separate from God. We are all part of God's energy and as such, receive His Love at all times.

There is nothing bad that you could possibly do that would keep you from receiving God's love. Conversely, there is also nothing you can do to earn special favor from God. God is love and can only give love. It is the purest form of love and

is extended equally to all in the universe as your inheritance.
Everyone is a part of the Sonship of God, and as such, you are
loved equally by God. Allow yourself to be identified with
who you are and not what you do so that you can receive all
that is yours to have.

Erroneous Belief 5:
You Must Do Something to Earn God's Forgiveness

Please understand that you have done nothing wrong that
requires forgiveness. God is only love, and as such, he sees
only love in his children, so there is nothing to forgive. All of
God's children, every man, woman, and child on this planet
here now, all of the people from the past, and those who will
be here in the future – will return to God in the place that you
call Heaven without exception. In reality, there is no need for
forgiveness, as there is only God's love in the universe.

Forgiveness doesn't exist in the heavenly realms, as it has
no purpose there. It is an earthly tool to aid you in reversing
your thinking and undoing your egoic mistakes. Forgiveness
allows your perceptions to be healed and errors corrected.
It is an opportunity for one to forgive oneself by forgiving
another. Offering forgiveness is the only way for you to have
it. Through forgiveness, you acknowledge the Christ in your
brothers and sisters and through them also in yourselves.
In essence, forgiveness corrects your false beliefs about the
world around you, as love needs no forgiveness.

God made us all in his likeness, and as such, you are love.
As a physical manifestation of God's energy, you are not
required to be perfect, because you already are. In your
physical incarnation, there are no requirements to do or
not do anything. Your soul is perfect love and incapable of
anything but love, and as such, cannot do anything wrong.
In the physical realm of Earth, your body can be directed by
your spirit self or your ego. Your physical consciousness has
free will and can choose to live from your soul self or your
egoic thought system. The choices the ego makes affect only
the body and what is located on the earthly plane of existence.

The choices the soul self makes can come only from love, making it incapable of sin and in no need of forgiveness.

You are human *beings*, not human doers. Every moment of every day, you make choices. These choices involve being or not being what you are currently being. If your choice is not to continue what you were being, then you can consider what you would like to *be* next. Each choice has an outcome of either feeling "good" or feeling "bad" about yourself coming from your previous actions. If you don't like the feeling that was the outcome of your previous choices, then the good news is that you get to choose again. If you continue actions that cause you to feel good as an outcome, you will be happy. If you choose actions that lead to negative emotions, then you will not. It really is that simple. As an outcome of all your thoughts, words, and deeds, you are 100 percent responsible for where you are right now and how your life will play out in the future.

Please remember that whenever you come from a place of love, your outcome will always be one of joy, peace, and harmony. Whenever you come from a place other than love, your outcome will be one of negative emotions such as fear, sorrow, regret, lament, anger, depression, jealousy, anxiety, blame, and others. It is Our hope that your choice will be to live from love so that you may experience the love, peace, and joy that flows back to you as an outcome of your loving actions. Understanding that you create your own reality from the choices you make is how you can grow spiritually. It is an ebb and flow of learning what "living from love" has to offer you in life.

Erroneous Belief 6:
You Are Inherently Evil in Nature and Require Control

You were born as perfect love and had a basal awareness of your natural state of Oneness. From your cultural upbringing and what you were taught by others in your homes and schools, you learned to reject or suppress this part of yourself. You learned to embrace only what could be seen in your physical world. Again, there is nothing wrong with what has occurred here. I am only pointing out what is true in your current world so that you may see what brought about these false beliefs. We wish for you to know your truth at this time.

The beliefs that you are inherently evil in nature and need to be controlled were founded in the chambers of power, from their fear of anarchy. During many periods in your history, there was much to fear. Humans were not living from love and at times were very far from that state of being. It was during these times that religions used their pulpits as a means to control the masses with their teachings so that peace could prevail. Because of the behaviors of some, many religious leaders preached of a god who would punish the people if they didn't adhere to the rules of their religion. Some religions created very harsh rules, whereas others were gentler in their approach. These rules came from certain periods in your history and what was occurring within those religions during that period of time. Fear is a huge motivator of people, but the result is quite different from living from love.

These rules were also strongly influenced by the personal experiences of the leaders who made up the rules and their beliefs about their own personal experiences. If they had negative experiences with women, then their rules reflected the belief that women were considered evil and needed to be suppressed, covered, or subservient. If they saw the negative effects of drinking, then they made rules that made drinking against God's laws. If they witnessed provocative dancing and others having fun when they couldn't, then those activities were also forbidden.

Again, there are no requirements from God that you act or not act in a certain way. This would be incongruent with you having free will. As I mentioned above, We hope that you will choose those behaviors that will bring you the highest and best outcome. We want what makes you happy. It brings Us such joy to observe you living in love, peace, honor, and excitement rather than sorrow, regret, depression, and the remaining long list of negative emotions.

Limiting Religious Beliefs

You will notice that much of what I discussed under the heading "Current Limiting Beliefs" can also be put here under a heading about religious beliefs. The reason I had them put under a more general heading about beliefs is that these concepts are for everyone, whether or not they believe in God or even practice a religion. These are universal truths even if you choose not to believe or even acknowledge them. These laws are universal laws just as gravity is a universal law in your world. You are at the mercy of these laws, just like physical laws, whether or not you know of or believe in their properties.

You are constantly moving toward love, so this process naturally moves you away from your old ways of being. They soon become unacceptable, as the purpose they served is no longer applicable. It is important that I reiterate that all paths lead to God. No one fails to be good enough, holy enough, or enough of anything else. Each and every being in the universe returns to God no matter your origin, religion, or the choices you make in life. Each human who comes to your planet eventually dies, and when that occurs, each person's spirit leaves its bodily confines and return to the spiritual realm. This is also a universal truth.

Within all that I have said previously, I can now speak to you of world religions. Most of your larger religions have roots that go back thousands of years. Most were initiated by ascended masters and messengers. During the initial stages of these religions, little was written down. Of the original writings, most were lost through the centuries because of war and pillage. Much of what is now in your Bible, Torah, Talmud, and other holy books is information that was passed from family to family and stories that were told from generation to generation. As these stories were retold, much of their original context was lost. By the time these stories were finally put into scrolls or books, the text had already changed many, many times. These changes were made because of forgetfulness, an unintentional misunderstanding of the stories, or an intentional addition of information. The intentional additions were an attempt to either explain the stories or to use them as a tool to control the followers.

Most of you have played the childhood game of telephone and experienced how stories told from person to person to person, within one room and only minutes apart, have changed until what was originally said was no longer discernible. I have used this example as a means for you to understand that much of the original facts and parables told thousands of years ago have been distorted through the telling and retelling. New information was inserted in just the same way as it occurs in the child's game. It is from this perspective that We ask you to consider that some portions of your religious documentation and dogma are not set in their original context. It was neither intended for you, nor does it serve you or your religions. I will begin by listing the most prevalent practices that no longer serve you and are still found across numerous religions.

1. You must behave in a certain way, avoiding "wrong" deeds, or you will not be allowed entry into the kingdom of heaven.

2. You must attend religious services, or you will not be allowed entry into the kingdom of heaven.

3. You must practice certain prayers at certain times of the day in order to enter into the kingdom of heaven.

4. Women cannot be leaders within a religion or become ministers, priests, rabbis, and so on; otherwise, it is a sin.

5. Church leaders cannot be married or have a sexual relationship with another person or it is a sin.

6. Sex is bad or should be performed for procreation only or it is a sin. Sex before marriage is a sin.

7. Children must be baptized in order to enter the kingdom of heaven.

8. You may eat only certain foods or it is a sin.

9. You may not drink, dance, wear certain clothing, or makeup or it is a sin.

I know reading this may be counter to some of your beliefs for those who practice religions. I ask only that you consider these beliefs to be erroneous. You are under no requirement to do so. You have a choice to accept what has been written here or not. You may accept all of it, some of it, or none of it. It is my hope that truth will prevail and you will open your hearts to the truths I have put here. I will address each of these beliefs individually as a means of explaining the original message and intent behind each message.

Erroneous Religious Belief 1:
You must behave in a certain way or avoid all "wrong" deeds or you will not be allowed entry into the kingdom of heaven.

This one belief has caused more inner turmoil for humans than any other religious rule ever spoken or written down in your history. It is at the center of all guilt, shame, regret, remorse, depression, and all other negative emotions. The truth is that you could commit the most heinous of crimes by your social standards and still return to the spiritual realm you call heaven, with no impact whatsoever. You will not be judged, nor will you have to pay a penance for thoughts, words, or actions you made while in the earthly realm. You are a spiritual being, a part of God, and as such, are incapable of anything but love. Any egoic, non-loving thoughts, words, or actions done while in the physical human manifestation are considered egoic mistakes and are left behind in the physical plane where the ego created them.

The reason I can tell you that everyone who incarnates on Earth returns to the heavenly realm without exception is that each of you at your core is a spirit that is a perfect part of God's energy. Since God is perfect, then you are perfect, because you are made up of God's energy, and this part of you is incapable of sin. The egoic thought system that has led the physical body to do things that were not of God's love remains in the physical plane at death. Only the soul energy lives on through infinity. All beings have a free will to choose to listen to the word of God or their ego. When you are listening to your ego, then your soul or spirit self is not engaged and is therefore not responsible for any thoughts, words, or actions

that the ego and physical body chooses. As you progress
spiritually in the physical realm, you will come to understand
that at times you have chosen unwisely and made a mistake.
When this occurs, turn to the Holy Spirit to ask him to correct
it, and in the asking, it will be given.

Although others do not judge you, upon your death you will
experience a life review from the perspective of each person
with whom you interacted. It is through this life review that
a soul learns and understands the truth of the effect their
choices have made on others while they walked your planet.
These life reviews are intended to assist help further learn and
understand how they can live more fully from love in future
incarnations. Each of you has the opportunity for spiritual
growth within each of your lifetimes, and that is the reason
you choose to incarnate within the physical planes.

Now that I've told you these major truths and shaken the
foundation of your beliefs, I will explain that Our wish for
you while you are on this planet is one of love, joy, peace,
unity, harmony, honor, and compassion. It is through living in
reflection of these emotions that you receive the benefits back
for yourself.

What you reap you sow.
It is by giving love that you receive love.
It is by giving joy that you receive joy.
It is by practicing peace that you maintain peace.
It is by living in harmony that you maintain harmony.
It is by living from honor that you receive honor.
It is by showing compassion that you receive compassion.

These are part of the spiritual laws of the Universe. This list
is by no means comprehensive but serves to explain to you
that what you do for or to another will ultimately return to
you. The good deeds return to you through good fortune. And
what you deem bad deeds return to you as negative results
within your life. It is the ultimate of cause and effect at work
in its purest form and is commonly referred to on your planet
as karma. Karma exists only in the physical plane and does
not exist in the heavenly realms. All of life is energy. And
energy must remain in balance in the physical realm, and

karma serves that purpose. You learn best of the effects of your own thoughts, words, and deeds when you actually have to experience them yourself.

Erroneous Religious Belief 2:
You must attend religious services or you will not be allowed entry into the kingdom of heaven.

Although you may wish to attend religious services as a means of reminding yourself that you are a child of God, there is no requirement from God for you to do so. This is by no means a suggestion to turn away from your religions or their practices. I am saying that to practice them is an individual choice. A choice that can help you become fully centered in your knowing you are as a child of God. In reality, it does not matter either way to God what you choose. It is your life to live in the manner best suited for you.

It is also important to note here that there is no place on this planet that is more holy than another place, as all that lives and that can be seen is from God's source. We are all part of God's energy, including the rocks, mountains, oceans, and all living beings on this planet. Thanking God for the beauty one sees while walking a forest path is no less heavenly a thanksgiving than one chanted while in a religious ceremony. God loves everyone and everything equally.

Additionally, all true prayers are heard and answered by God no matter the manner in which they are placed. Please understand that all manner of negative wishes or requests are NOT heard by God, as he is only love and can only hear loving thoughts. However, our negative thoughts and actions do play out in the spiritual laws of cause and effect as karma. With that said, it is recommended that you choose wisely what you think, say, do, or hope for another, as you are really requesting it for yourself. This is what was meant by the biblical saying, "Do unto others as you would have them do unto you." Since We are all made up of God's energy, and We are all connected as part of this energy, then whatever you do for another you are ultimately doing to yourself.

Erroneous Religious Belief 3:
You must practice certain prayers and/or pray at certain
times of the day in order to enter the kingdom of heaven.

As mentioned above, there is no requirement that a prayer must be said, let alone during a specific time of day or facing a certain direction. You may wish to pray this way as a manner of respect for your God or the ascended masters who founded your religion, but any mandated requirement to do so serves no relative purpose in and of itself within heaven or the spiritual realm. It does not matter to God in any way whether you do this or not, as everyone returns to the heavenly realm.

While We are discussing prayer, I will mention that your prayers can take many forms including requests for help, thanksgiving, healing, wants, and needs. In reality, God does not hear your prayers; he feels only the emotions in your heart. It is only the loving intent of your prayer that is heard. In fact, most of you pray for something or someone. There is nothing right or wrong in that. It is merely what occurs. The most frequent prayers said are typically one-sided conversations where you request something, then sit back and wait for your prayers to be answered. A prayer for God to hear is one with good intentions and a win/win for all involved. Know that prayer is the medium of miracles. Through prayer, love is received, and through love, it is expressed in miracles.

There are other ways to request assistance that are not currently being considered. Conversations with your Guardian Angels or Spirit Guides can assist you with making choices that will lead you to where you want to be. They may also provide insights into what is really taking place in any given situation so that you may choose to see the situation in a different light. You can now view these events in a way that honors each of the beings involved. These spiritual conversations can become a daily event for you if you so choose. They can allow you to move away from your egoic thought system, which has made up stories about what is occurring in your life. The insights of your angels, spirit guides, your spirit self, and your loved ones who have passed to the other side can allow you to move back into the light of truth and to live in peace and harmony with those around you.

Erroneous Religious Belief 4:
Women cannot be leaders within a religion or become ministers, priests, or rabbis, and so on, or it is a sin.

These rules are a source of sadness for Us to observe on this side of the veil. There is no intent to insult here, but in your history men have typically been the least able to lead from their spiritual self in many environments. In the history of Earth, females were the original spiritual leaders in all cultures. Throughout the subsequent generations, many egoic-minded and jealous men used their physical might to take over and control females. Through this continued domination, the females of your species have been repressed and controlled for thousands of years. This is not what God intended and should not be allowed to continue. As you are all individuations of God, would you tell God that he couldn't be a religious leader because he was manifested into a female body? Please understand that in reality, your Godliness has no gender.

It would probably be a good place here to explain what I mean when I say women were the original leaders. The first time you incarnated into physical existence, you came here as a male. (This also holds true for all species on all planets.) Within the ascension process, one must incarnate as a man first for numerous lifetimes before one matures to a spiritual level in which one may become a female. This is a spiritual truth and is intended for the survival of the species. The spirit self must evolve to a certain spiritual level to care for and nurture the offspring of the species.

Once you have become a female and matured in spirituality, you may choose to become either male or female in subsequent lives. It is all part of the master plan for spiritual development for those who choose to incarnate into the physical plane. It was done this way because females give birth, rear their offspring, and need to have a certain level of maturity to *be* and to maintain love, intuition, patience, and wisdom.

Within the female and male species, there are varying levels of spiritual maturity as well. In some cases, those who have reincarnated multiple times within their gender are at a more advanced level than others who have not. These rules are not steadfast, because each being may mature at different rates and through many spiritual levels in any given lifetime or not at all. It is a manner of free will and having the desire to live more spiritually.

Because of the different levels of spiritual maturity in male humans, some may not be as advanced as women. Those who are still spiritually immature aren't able to create from a place of love, peace, and harmony. Most males who live from their egos have neither the wisdom nor the spiritual experience to make sound decisions. Unfortunately, many egoic men are drawn to leadership to bolster their self-esteem. That is why you have experienced so much war and strife throughout periods of your history where egoic men have been the dominant leaders.

With that said, some of the greatest leaders in your history have been women. Many led your greatest advanced societies. Now, because women have been dominated and suppressed throughout history, most females on your planet are unaware of their innate abilities for great leadership. In your recent history, there has been little opportunity for women to participate at the highest levels of governments. It is important to note here that where women have risen to positions of leadership, those who have achieved greatness have led from their spirit selves with love, peace, and intuition. Those who were not good leaders led from their egoic thought systems.

Women can become great leaders if they are allowed the space and support to lead. They can provide much insight and perspective through their advanced intuition, which some men are unaware is available to them. So please, by all means, allow your women the opportunity to lead and participate fully in all positions available within your religions and governments. Your experience of knowing God through them will be better for it. We call to women to support other women to run for offices, and We ask men to support them as well. Look for those who are spiritually advanced, as they will make their decisions from their spirit selves and reflect the love, honor, and compassion needed to be great leaders.

The fact is that there is a great imbalance of male/female essence in your world, and it is your responsibility to bring it back into balance. Please understand that this information is not meant to show favoritism toward women, as some of your great leaders have been men also. These great men were matured souls who led from their spirit selves, with love, peace, compassion, and harmony as their guiding principles. Our wish is that you will mature to understand that males and females are equal in all ways and that there is no benefit of one over the other. The true measure of a leader is how wisely and lovingly they lead while making the right choices for the highest and best outcome for all involved.

Erroneous Religious Belief 5:
Church leaders cannot be married or have a sexual relationship with another person, or it is a sin.

Church leaders are those who are called to do spiritual work. Limiting their choices as to how that occurs is not what God intended. Each spiritual leader should be allowed to choose what experience they would like to have during this lifetime, no matter their occupation. Although an individual may choose to be celibate as a means by which to experience their path, it was never intended to be a mandated requirement for them to practice their religions. In fact, none of your early religious leaders of any of the faiths were celibate.

It does not matter to God what choice one makes in their religious experience here. Many of your religious leaders could become better leaders as an outcome of having lived through intimate experiences as husbands, wives, fathers, and mothers. Why would you want to limit a being who has chosen a spiritual path to one on which they are unable to experience all that they might otherwise choose to experience? In addition, this would include dating. Within the realm of dating and marriage, there would be courtship and sexual relationships. All of these practices are natural to the human species and a part of the process of getting

to know one another. It is a special means by which to
understand compatibilities between the individuals. As long
as the individuals are acting from a place of love, respect,
compassion, and responsibility, then what harm could prevail
to prevent them from being in a natural union with each
other? It does not matter to God whether a religious leader
is married or single, cohabitates or not. It is all a matter of
individual choice.

Erroneous Religious Belief 6:
Sex is bad or should be performed only for procreation, or it is a sin. Sex before marriage is a sin.

These rules have caused many good people to be burdened by
guilt, remorse, shame, and fear. It has led to anger, self-denial,
and many psychological disorders through the displaced
guilt, shame, and fear. Sex is a very natural act. It was never
intended to be overshadowed by guilt and shame. God never
required that sex be intended for procreation only. Nor did
God intend for men and women to be married to engage in
sex. These beliefs were created by the egoic mind, because
it believed that God required something from us. In an effort
to appease God, some religious leaders decided that giving
up sex, which is the highest pleasure of the physical realm,
would surely do the trick. In reality, it does not matter to
God if, when, how, or why you engage in sex. We ask that
it be performed in a respectful, loving, compassionate, and
responsible way.

Sex is a beautiful act of love and attraction. It is something
that both parties should thoroughly enjoy. It is a want to
give and receive mutual pleasure. It is an expression of love
coming from a physical and spiritual attraction. Please stop
teaching your children that sex is bad. Your prisons are full
of those who have much guilt and shame around sexuality.
Sex is one of the ultimate expressions of love. Why must your
egos make it into something that is wrong or negative? By all
means, please practice safe sex and use birth control methods
so that there is no concern for an unwanted pregnancy. This
is a wise practice, as your world population is growing at a
rate that will be difficult to sustain in the near future. When

engaging in mutual, consensual sex, treat each other with respect and tenderness, and act with the intention of the highest and best outcome for each other.

Erroneous Religious Belief 7:
Women must be covered to be in a church or out in public, or it is a sin.

God has never required anyone to wear certain clothing. It does not matter to God if a person is clothed or unclothed or the manner in which one is dressed. We recognize that your current social mores require people to wear clothing, and there is no judgment one way or another for these rules. We are merely pointing out that there is no requirement from God to do so. Your bodies are a thing of beauty and should not be covered up in shame. These teachings fall into the categories of beliefs that were inserted into original teachings and messages. Although there may be a physical need for certain types of clothing for certain weather conditions on your planet, these are merely preferences or choices from your societies.

There are also many societies on your planet that require women to wear clothing that covers their entire body, and they are punished when this does not occur. These rules were originally designed to protect women from marauding bands of thieves and rapists. Unfortunately, these rules made their way into their religions as well. Again, We would ask that you consider changing these rules so that the women of your societies can enjoy their rightful unencumbered, equal place in society and religions. You would do right by allowing them to make whatever choices they wish to make in all situations and cease to make it wrong in your societies.

Erroneous Religious Belief 8:
You must be baptized to enter the kingdom of heaven.

Everyone born into a physical body is a perfect being. Each of you is born pure of mind and spirit, and does not require any religious ceremony to enter the kingdom of heaven. As mentioned previously, everyone who manifests into a physical body will return to the place that they never left, no matter what occurs to them or by them in this or any other lifetime. It does not matter to God if you are baptized or not.

Although baptism symbolizes cleansing and a commitment to be on your spiritual path, one does not have to be baptized to be cleansed or committed to their spiritual path. If parents wish to baptize their child as a means of showing support for their religion, then by all means they should do so. However, please do not place the stigma on them that they will not be able to enter into the kingdom of God unless they do so.

All children of God will return to the spiritual realm, the place they never left, upon their death, and there is nothing anyone must or must not do for this to occur. The reality is that none of you has ever left the spirit realm. You are triune beings existing as a soul with a human body and mind. Your spirit selves are continuously in union with God during your human experience on your planet. Once you have remembered this about yourselves, you will be able to open yourselves up to the full powers of your true self.

Erroneous Religious Belief 9:
You may eat only certain foods, or it is a sin.

This rule is also not from God. These types of rules were originally contrived as a means of protecting the masses from eating harmful foods and have no context in your world religions today. Some of these rules were originally based upon ways of protecting people from unhealthful food preparation and practices. They served the community as a means of protection in those times in history. They could have been written as social rules, but the leaders during those times created them as religious ones because the people were more easily manipulated through religious laws than if they had originated from their civil leaders. There was no harm intended in the act of writing these rules; they were intended only for the protection of the people. We merely ask that you see them for what they are and understand their origin. Although you may choose to eat organic or kosher foods or restrict yourself from eating certain food products, it is not now, nor will it ever be, a requirement by God. Your diet should always come from self-love and not fear.

You will return to the spirit realm no matter what you consume in your lifetime. If you wish to choose to experience restricted diets, then by all means enjoy that state of being. Please let go of the guilt and the thought of punishment if you should choose to eat or drink what others or certain religions feel you should not. What you do is an individual preference. When you no longer want to experience the consequences of ingesting foods that may not be good for you, then you are free to choose otherwise at any time. We ask religions to please step away from infringing on the rights of others to choose the experience each wishes to have in the here and now of physical life.

Erroneous Religious Belief 10:
You may not drink or dance or wear certain clothing or makeup, or it is a sin.

Again, We are dealing with rules that were laid down as a means to control the masses. None of these rules came from God. They were introduced into religious documents as a means to control behaviors. Most rules and beliefs were added with good intentions. They came from social beliefs that were passed down from generation to generation. Many believed chaos would prevail if these rules were not included in their religious doctrines, so they included them with thoughts that they were doing what was right at the time. Although there may have been much drinking and cavorting going on during periods of your history, these rules have done little to suppress those behaviors. Through observation, it would be easy to say that some of these behaviors do not serve the individuals well, but that is not for anyone to judge. These are not God's laws but merely moral codes to control the masses.

Although societies may wish to have rules about certain behaviors, breaking these rules does not lead anyone away from God. God does not care what you eat or drink or if you sing or dance. You are free to choose the experience you wish to have while you are here on Earth. You will return to the place you never left no matter what choices you make while here on Earth. No one is wrong here, neither the people who wrote these rules into religious doctrines nor those who did not follow them. Make a point to come from love to determine what choices resonate for you, and follow those.

Please understand that this list of erroneous beliefs is by no means comprehensive, but serves the purpose of bringing to your awareness that which no longer serves you. These beliefs have caused many on your planet to suffer the shame and guilt of being judged by others for experiencing these actions. Remember that karmic law says that as you judge others, so you shall be judged by others. In reality, you will judge only yourself. As always, it is your decision to embrace letting go of these erroneous beliefs or not, but know that nothing will keep you from having the love of God and returning to the heavenly realm."

Governmental Beliefs

The original societies on your planet remembered who they were and didn't require many laws. Unfortunately, this way of living did not prevail in your history. Governments around your world have ruled through the egoic wants of personal power and control since the earliest times on your planet. As the egoic thought systems became the prevalent means of controlling your physical actions, more and more laws were deemed necessary and more restrictive.

Throughout your history, We have heard many prayers requesting assistance for how governments are led. In response, We have sent many messengers to assist you with the creation of better ways of living. Unfortunately, these periods of better living have been relatively short lived. Within your third-dimension realm where egoic thoughts prevailed, power, greed, and control have followed. Where there are thoughts of power, greed, and control, love, peace, and harmony cannot be present. Know that these types of negative behaviors will occur less and less as your planet evolves to become a fourth-, and then a fifth-dimensional planet.

Recently in your history, in answer to many prayers, We
assisted the newly elected United States leaders in creating
the foundation for their government and judicial systems.
The original design of the United States federal government
created a framework of laws of the people, by the people,
and for the people. It was intended to lead the nation toward
a fifth-dimensional Oneness. Although the system worked
with good intentions for several hundred years, it has veered
significantly off the path from what was originally intended.
The original Constitution, which was Divinely guided, has
systematically been eroded, becoming a means for control of
the many by the wealthy few.

In its purest form, the U.S. Constitution was designed to
provide the framework for ruling a country of dissimilar
states. It was designed to protect the rights of the individual
as well as to establish a mechanism for guiding social
consciousness. Through trust, common interests, and
conscious forethought, the states voted to join the union of
states. The union allowed all to benefit from the strength of
the whole.

Unfortunately, the purity of the original Constitution is
now gone and has been replaced with new "interpretations"
allowing for corruption and greed. Through special interests,
legislators have allowed the US government to be influenced
by those with controlling purposes. Through monetary,
"influence," your original laws have been changed or
reinterpreted to place the burden of social consciousness onto
the middle and lower classes of people. Your Oneness way of
life is no longer protected by your governments.

Unfortunately, for your world today, in most cases issues of
social consciousness are focused upon only by nonprofits
and religious groups. It used to be that the USA was the last
holdout for truth and justice for all, but that is no longer the
case. We do not wish to place the USA in a bad light, and this
is not an exclusive USA issue by any means. We had hoped
that the USA could serve as a model for the rest of the world.
It would take much change to reverse the changes made to the
original intent for this to be the case moving forward. In the
near future, as your world moves closer to Oneness, the USA

may choose to take the lead once again to correct the errors of the past. Your US leaders can choose at any time to bring their nation back into balance with all of life, and in doing so, they can once again become an example for others to follow."

Corruption and Greed

Upon ushering in the new world, you will no longer tolerate the corruption and greed that is so prevalent in your world today. Through your concerns about what is occurring on your planet, you will begin to insist upon change. You will learn of the many power-seekers who are looking to take control of many of the essential resources on your planet. You will see that through their self-interest, they have chosen a path of power, greed, and corruption and have thus far manipulated many of your world's monetary and banking systems. Once you begin to investigate, you will also find that they have influenced your governments, your media, and the companies that provide you with the goods that you consume.

As more and more people awaken, they will begin to realize that their rights and freedoms have slowly been eroded without much resistance. We thank those who have been diligent in trying to educate you about what is occurring. Once you realize what is really happening, your ego may begin to run amok with thoughts of conspiracy and potential war. But these thoughts will only bring fear to you and not serve you well. Stay well grounded in loving thoughts, as fear causes people to make decisions that do not serve them, in either the short or the long term. Be mindful that fearful thoughts will attract more fear, and that will not serve you either. You wouldn't want to spread fear, as it may lead to worse or elongated outcomes.

The more you are coming from a place of love and wanting to serve and help others, the more you will be able to calm the political storms. I know this might sound counter to what makes sense, but you can change what is occurring while still coming from a loving and caring frame of mind. Think of Gandhi and Martin Luther King and how they appeared and led groups to make changes in extreme conditions. Their cultures endured many adverse conditions, but they still managed to bring about major peaceful changes from within the system as a result. They did so through coordinated, peaceful protests and by using the existing law-changing processes within their respective countries.

The old ways of governing will fall away in the new world. New changes will be shepherded in through loving and positive avenues. The avenue of least resistance is made manifest when change comes from within the current system. If you should choose to become politically involved with those who are supporting actions to heal your planet and political systems, We ask that you do so only in peaceful and positive ways. There are many groups in numerous countries that are banding together to assist those who wish to become involved in a peaceful manner. Please be diligent in your search for a peaceful group to support, as there are many false groups set up by the power brokers. You will know the right group by their guiding principles and peaceful actions to bring about change and lawful remediation. Remember that all violent and nonpeaceful actions play into the power brokers' plans and could cause a more devastating impact on this planet. Stay away from any groups or rogue factions from within legitimate groups that are planning nonpeaceful actions. Also, stay away from those groups that are coming from fear, hate, or other negative emotions.

We are protecting you in ways you cannot imagine and have done so through many periods in your history. Most of these protections will be unseen, but have faith that they are there for you. Your most important role throughout all this is to remain in the emotion of love and to help others do the same. Genuinely living in the emotion of love will smooth the way for the peaceful transition of power from the few elite to the many.

Governments are meant to serve the good of all and to protect the planet. Step back and see how far your planet has moved from these concepts. Decide to make the changes that will bring your countries back into alignment with the true role of any government, one that is of service to all. There is much work to do to bring your planet back into balance with nature and the Universe. Please consider using these basic guidelines as a means to establish a course of action to take you into your intended future as a planet of perpetual peace.

It is Our hope for you that the current shifts of energy coming into your planet will allow the majority of you to advance spiritually. If that is your desire, then your spirit self will become the dominant thought system for you and will lead you in the direction of love and peace. Within your new spirituality, you may also wish to look to form new laws that will allow you to bring your governments back into balance. To keep corruption out of your realigned governments, you may also wish to enact laws that prevent any officials from benefiting in any way from their position of power.

Pay your leaders well for their services, and they will be less likely to consider corrupt thoughts. Go back to the basic concepts of government and leadership. Choose your leaders carefully by giving the most weight to their spiritual maturity. Determine if they actually live their lives in Oneness. Observe them to see if they are coming from a place of love and want what is best for all concerned. Do they support what is of the highest and best benefit for all on your planet? If not, then perhaps you will want to support those who do live from love and Oneness, beginning now. Start by encouraging those public officials who have made an important difference at the local level to seek positions that are more advanced. Push those who have served humanity with honor and compassion up the ladders of your governments.

Social Mores

Another area We would ask you to look at as you ascend is how your societies are living and interacting with each other. The social mores on your planet vary widely, depending upon the country, location, and religion of your family of origin. So much in your world is now influenced by media giants, schools, music, and religions. The numbing of generations of children through TV, movies, games, drugs, and negative music has caused your societies to lose connection with each other. Some of you have come to believe that obtaining material goods and looking good to others is how to attain happiness and love. How sad it is for Us to observe such suffering and sadness when it is all so unnecessary.

Please consider the many "dos and don'ts" in your societies that make little sense. We see so many judged by what they wear and drive, where they live, what job they have, and on and on. People are judged on so many levels that there is little room in your lives for the personal connections and love that was intended for you. Please look past the advertisements and products to see the greed in the corporations sitting in the background controlling all that you see and have in your world.

It is okay to want things, and there is nothing wrong with that, but the judgment that surrounds the "haves" and the "have-nots" is ripping your societies apart. Please understand that when you judge another, you are also judging yourself. And then you have to live up to the rules of your own judgments. While you judge others with made-up stories about them, you are also acting as their jailer. This is your egoic mind at its height of insanity. Why would you label another when you would not want that label perpetrated upon yourself? Remember that what you wish or make present for another will be mirrored back to you from the universe.

You have all heard, "As you judge so shall you be judged." Although you will not now, or ever be judged by God, your egoic judgments of others are reflected to you, as others will then judge you. Please let go of judgment. It is like a plague to your societies and does not serve you. It serves only to move you further away from the peace, love, joy, connectedness, and happiness you want so very much in your lives. Remember it is through forgiveness of these judgments that healing can take place. As you go through the process of forgiving others, you will also be forgiven by those you have judged. In truth, you are judging and then forgiving yourself.

The path to happiness is paved with peace, joy, love, acceptance, and serving others. It is through serving and embracing others that you receive peace, joy, compassion, honor, and excitement in your lives. What you do for another will come back to you from the universe. Does it not make sense to be of service rather than to send out negative thoughts and actions that will be mirrored back to you?

To begin healing your planet you may want to ask yourselves these questions:

Where has the social consciousness of your societies gone?
What has happened to the belief that what is good for the whole of the planet is what is best for each nation?
Where is your social consciousness in businesses, governments, schools, and religions?
Who will speak for the lesser of those in your communities?
If not you, then who?

We gently ask you to remember who you really are so you can begin the process of healing all that is around you. Bringing your planet, societies, governments, and religions back into balance will not be an easy task. The first step is the realization that what is currently occurring is not working. The second step is determining what changes need to take place and in what priority. The third step is taking the actions necessary to bring about the associated changes. For those who have been listening to their voice of God, these changes will be nothing more than a speed bump. Some will have a difficult time understanding these changes, for they are holding on to fears and thoughts of scarcity. Consider becoming a change agent and get involved in healing your societies, countries, and planet. All your loving efforts will bring you closer to the fifth dimension.

During these times of change and uncertainty, make a conscious decision to embrace the inherent goodness in each of your fellow travelers on their journey. Each person who comes into your life is there for a reason. Release any judgments of others first, then of yourself. Forgiveness allows you to move out of your ego and live from your spirit self. It is a very freeing process and can unburden you of all the negative emotions you carry from your past as well. Go backward in your memory to your earliest childhood and then progress forward. Forgive each person who has ever hurt you, and then send him or her loving kindness. Once you start seeing your fellow travelers in this way, you will be on the right path to healing yourselves and living in Oneness. It is from this perspective that lasting change can occur."

Time for Change

Changing the false beliefs and embracing the truth of who you really are is the foundation to understanding Oneness. As each person awakens to embrace his or her Divinity, the world moves one step closer to *being* in Oneness. It is through living in loving kindness that God can be found in all that is around you. Once you have awakened, then you begin to feel the urge and need to be of service to others using your natural talents, qualities, and abilities. Channel these awakened urges into work that will benefit others, your communities, and your planet.

Enlightenment, peace, joy, love, kindness, gentleness, humor, honesty, excitement, compassion, and honor are your intended states of being. They will lead to positive outcomes of more and more peace, love, and joy within your lives. This is your true circle of life. Live your life with peace and love while you enjoy all that you have come here to experience. And in doing so, your experience here will be full of honor, compassion, and excitement. We send you blessings as you walk your path back to God.

Universal Laws are those laws that affect all energy within the Divine Universe.

Chapter 4
Universal Laws

Universal Laws

Universal laws are those laws that affect all energy within the Divine Universe, which is the All That Is. Since We are all a part of God's energy, We are all affected by these laws, whether or not you believe in God or these laws. Gravity is a natural law of your planet. It doesn't matter whether you know of these laws or not or believe in them or not, you are affected by them. It is important to understand this as you read and learn more about your physical existence on Earth and who you are as a child of God.

It also behooves one to understand these universal truths in depth so that you can live intentionally and use these laws to your benefit. Please understand that these laws are merely a small subset of the universal laws and are listed here because they are the ones that affect your planet the most at this time. Some of these have been mentioned earlier in this book but are mentioned here again to draw attention to their importance.

We Are All One with God

All that is in the universe is one with God and includes all of the seen and unseen. In the beginning, there was only God, and He was known only to Himself. Then God wanted to more fully experience who He was while in relationship to others. To come to know this, God created All That Is in what your scientists have referred to as the "big bang." In this one sacred moment, God created All That Is from His own sacred God energy. The process of life, as you know it on your planet, is a recurring process of that original energy being transformed between the physical and the nonphysical realms over and over again.

All that is physical, including the planets, rocks, oceans, rivers, mountains, plants, animals, sea creatures, and humans, as well as all higher beings in the heavenly realms, are made up of God's energy. This energy is in a constant dance between the physical and nonphysical planes and is how God comes to know Himself. It is within your experiences that God comes to know and experience Himself more fully again and again. It is through evil that God knows goodness. It is through fear that God can more closely know love. And these contrasting opposites in which you experience different emotions bring deeper meaning into your lives. These experiences allow you to grow spiritually as you learn how to become an individuation of God's love during your many lifetimes of physical manifestation.

We Are All Energy

Everything in the universe is made up of Divine energy. All of the solar systems, suns, planets, nebulas, black holes, and all that you have yet to discover are made up of this energy. This includes everything living, from one-cell beings to the largest living creatures on your planet. It also includes the plants, trees, rivers, lakes, and seas. The Divine energy also includes the smallest subatomic particles and the smaller yet-to-be discovered particles, your Himalayan Mountains, and everything within Earth. You are all a part of the Universal Consciousness of God and His Divine Energy.

All that you see, including everything you make from the resources on your planet, is also part of the Divine Energy. The denser the object, the slower its energy is vibrating. Rock and Earth are very dense and appear to be inert, but when one looks upon them at the microscopic level, one can see the movement from within. The less dense or higher-frequency objects can move more easily within the universe. The highest-frequency energies cannot be seen by the human eye but are real nonetheless.

In order to physically manifest into your human body, your
energy must be concentrated and its frequency slowed down
to the appropriate level of density for human existence.
For those born onto your planet, this occurs at the time of
conception, and their energy continues to accumulate and
concentrate through the human growth processes. A similar
process occurs for animals and plants as well. The energy that
creates everything is all a part of the Divine Energy and has
chosen to show up as it appears to you now. This energy is
here to assist you in having the experience you wished to have
before manifesting in this lifetime."

We Are All Connected

All energy is interconnected, as We are all part of the Divine
Energy. Although you may appear disconnected through
your human eyes, your energy has neither a beginning nor
an ending. It is continuous and flows from person to person,
person to animal, person to rock, person to water, person to
planet, and on through to all the other potential matrixes of
connection points for each manifestation of energy in the
universe. It is through this interconnectedness that each of
you is able to fully experience your Oneness.

By connecting into the Universal Divine Consciousness, you
will find the knowledge of your purpose for being on this
planet at this monumental time in your history. Learn to plug
into this consciousness to see all that is available to you to
know and experience while you are here. It is always available
to you and part of what makes you a triune being. There are
several ways to make a connection to the Universal Divine
Consciousness, and they will be covered in other chapters.

You Are Triune Beings

In your physical manifestation, you are made up of three
things: spirit, mind, and body. Your spirit enfolds your body
and continues outward around you. Approximately two to
three feet above your head is your mind. All your thoughts
emanate from your mind, which is contained in your skull.

It is your brain, which stores thoughts and memories coming from your mind. Think of your mind as your computer processor and your brain as a computer storage device, as that is the best way to describe it. Your brain also places large stores of memories within the cellular structure throughout your body.

Your mind is that which gives you thoughts. It is not within your physical body. Remember that your brain is that part of your body that records thoughts, action, feelings, and experiences within its memory and other areas of the body. The brain also controls and regulates your body per the input your mind gives it. Your thoughts can be controlled either through your human-derived ego or your spirit self. The lower egoic brain knows only of its human existence, and as such, does not understand or know of the soul's presence. It is aware there is something else it should know but inherently doesn't know what it is. That is why your ego makes up stories about what is occurring around you. Your ego is concerned only with survival and doesn't understand your world. Therefore, your ego tries to understand it through these stories. It invents stories in an attempt to keep it from the fears of the unknown. When you live from your spirit self, your ego will no longer need to make up information to understand the world. You will now be informed through the Universal Divine Knowledge that is available to your spirit self.

Your spirit or soul is that part of you that is connected to the Universal Consciousness of God. It has the ability to tap into the Universal Divine Knowledge that is available to all in the universe. You have this ability whether or not you know you do or believe you do. It can be tapped into at any time you wish by conscious intent. It lies dormant within you until such time that you wish to remember and learn how to use it. To tap into it, you must raise your vibrational level to match that of the Divine Universal Consciousness.

Your spirit also has the ability to connect to those on the other side of the veil any time it wishes. The connection manifests from thought and can be made through raising your vibrations to match that of the one with whom you wish to communicate. It really is as simple as that. The difficulty that most of you have in making this connection lies in the belief that you can no longer have a relationship with those who have passed. It is this thought that they are lost to you that is manifested into the lack of communication.

Your thoughts control your perpetual experience while in a body and within the spirit realm as well. Your mind chooses the experiences that it wishes you to have, and then through the law of attraction manifests them into your life. Once you are purposefully living life through your spirit self, your ego will cease in its role as the decision maker. You will then begin to live an intentional life that manifests from your loving, purposeful thoughts.

Your physical body is the manifestation of your soul's desire to have the human experience at this time on your planet. You chose this time in your Earth's history to be a part of the most advanced leap in human evolution since the early times on your planet. All who are on the planet at this time have chosen to experience being a part of this wonderful advancement in the human evolution. Many have not awakened as of yet, so they do not know this is their purpose.

Others, and there will be many, may choose to lay their body down before or during this new shift in consciousness. They will lay their body down for various reasons, but most will choose to do so because they have completed what they have come here to do in this lifetime. Others might be called to lay their body down because they can be of more service from the other side of the veil. It may be easier for you to understand their passing by realizing that they have done so as a completion of this lifetime. They are now available to move forward into their next spiritual experience.

God Is Only Love

God is love and God can only be love. As you are part of God, you are also love. This is the universal law that can be used to explain many of the other universal laws. It is through God's love that We connect to the Divine universe. His Love asks for nothing and gives everything. It is constant and eternal.

He is the creator of the All and All was created from Him by Him. Since everything was created by Him, from Him, All That Is, is love. As We are God's energy and part of the All of God's Sonship, We are also pure love. You may perceive you are other things, but in reality, each of you is only love.

Free Will

As incarnations of God, you are endowed with creation and free will. Your free will was given to you to joyfully create your heart's desire. Within your free will, you may choose to move in the direction of your ascension or you may choose to follow a different path. The spirit self lovingly guides you in the direction of your ascension, and your ego fearfully deflects you away from it. The path of ascension lovingly leads you in the direction of harmony and peace with All That Is on your planet. It is always your choice as to which voice you wish to listen to. When you are living from the egoic thought system, fear leads you away from the truth of who you are. When you listen to the voice of love, you are on the path of freedom from fear and moving toward love and joy in your life.

Cause and Effect

The law of cause and effect is operating at all times in the physical universe, whether or not you believe in or are aware or unaware of its existence. Cause and effect does not exist in the spiritual realm, as love creates only love. In the physical realm, for every effect there must be a cause. Each of you is 100 percent of the cause of all that is around you, all that has occurred to you, and what you experience each day. Your ability to create and miscreate depends entirely upon the source of your thoughts, words, and actions. You create from love and miscreate through fear. Your ego leads the way for miscreation and your spirit self creates out of love. The mastery of cause and effect is through love.

This is a difficult law for many to understand. Some of you believe that others are the cause of your problem and that you are the victim of their pursuits. This is the core of misunderstanding for many. Some of you confuse the effect for the cause, and as such, you don't realize that you have created all that occurs to and for you. You may ask how that is possible, and I would respond by telling you that your thoughts, words, and deeds manifest for you. If your thoughts, words, and deeds come from love, then your world reflects that love to you. If you are living out of your egoic mind, then your thoughts, words, and deeds will be a reflection of fear, and your life will find fear reflected to you in what occurs for you.

To fully understand, you must realize the true power of thought to avoid miscreation out of fear. In your past, some of you have been fearful of everything and everyone. There are those who are afraid of God, of Me, and of themselves. In your misperception, you have miscreated God into something We are not. Your conflict is really between creation and miscreation, or better put, between love and fear. By choosing love to create your thoughts, words, and actions, you reject fear and manifest beauty in your lives. If you create from your egoic thought system, you produce fear and manifest negative events in your life.

Karmic Law

Karmic law says that whatever you do for another, you also do for yourself. If you send love, joy, and peace out into the world, then you will receive love, joy, and peace back from the world. It is the balancing nature of cause and effect. If you hurt or harm someone else or act in an unloving way to another, then the universe will mirror that to you as part of karmic law. How another treats you is reflected in their karma, and how you react to them is mirrored back in yours. What comes back to you doesn't necessarily come back to you from the person who was the object of your positive or negative thoughts, words, or deeds. But it will come back to you nonetheless. In addition, the mirrored karma may not happen right away and may take a long period of time to reflect to you.

Karmic laws exist only in the physical realms. There is no karmic law in the spiritual realm, as there is no need for it. The universe balances all energy with like energy coming back to you from all your thoughts, words, and actions. This occurs for each person on your planet. If your karma is not balanced out in your current lifetime when you die, then you will have either positive or negative or both karmic energies awaiting you in your future lifetime. This is how you learn and grow spiritually.

Most learn about karmic lessons while they are still young through the positive and negative experiences of living life with others. You typically find out early in life that whenever you do something harmful to another, there are unpleasant consequences to that behavior, and you immediately cease to practice these behaviors again. But there are those who continue to do the same actions again and again and remain oblivious to the laws of cause/effect and to the recurring strife and drama that comes back to them.

Pay attention to what you wish to have happen for yourself and others. If you live your life through love and truly work for the highest good for all of those around you, then you will experience many positive events in your life. When you continue to see evil in everyone and react to them from within that space, then you are going to have many negative experiences in your life. The more you believe the world is evil, the more evil will show up in your life. If you want to change your life, then change your thoughts about your life.

Once you realize that each person who shows up in your life is there for either a karmic or a Divine reason, then you can appreciate them more fully for the role they play in each experience you have. They are assisting you in spiritual learning, such that once learning is complete, all associated negative karma is released. Understanding that most people who come into your lives are there to provide you with your mirrored previous thoughts, words, or deeds can assist you in learning from and clearing past karma. These can be either positive or negative karma releases and may have come from this or a previous lifetime.

There Is No Need for Forgiveness

There is no need for forgiveness, because God does not perceive anything other than love. Since God is only love, He can only give love. He does not judge anyone or anything; it is not possible, as it is not a part of love. You are a part of God and come from pure love, too. Your spirit self does not recognize good and evil and does not judge others either. Unfortunately, this is not true of your egoic mind. Any time you judge another, you are doing so from your egoic mind.

Many of you were taught to believe in good and evil, and that God punishes those who are evil. You were also taught that you must follow God's laws or you will not enter heaven. These are false beliefs and portray God as something He is not. Because you have a free will and have beliefs in good and evil, you judge yourselves and others through your thoughts, words, and actions. Then you punish yourself and/or others for their thoughts, words, and actions. You make yourselves and others feel wrong, shameful, and unworthy of love. It is all so unnecessary and takes you away from the love that you crave. You have merely made a mistake that calls for correction. Ask the Holy Spirit to assist you in correcting your mistake. And when the learning and the correction is complete, the negative karma is released.

Let go of judgment of yourselves and others, as it does not serve you. It only brings about friction, hate, and a long list of other negative emotions. Also through cause and effect, it continues to create a cycle of judgment going out from you, which then must come back to you through karma judgment from others. Through the healing power of forgiveness, you can learn to end judgment in your lives and move closer to the life that was intended for you. Being mindful of your thoughts is the key to moving from your circular state of judgment and forgiveness. Remember that unconditional love does not judge, so there is no need for forgiveness.

Death Does Not Exist

Death is a concept that few of you truly understand, for in reality, it does not exist. You are not your body; you are a soul that has chosen to incarnate into a body. Although you appear as a separate body, you are pure energy, and as such, you have always been and will continue to be pure energy for all of eternity. You are all a part of God's energy, which does not dissipate and is ever expanding. All That Is in the universe is God's energy, and you are forever a part of that energy.

Death is a made-up concept derived early in your history as a means of explaining how a manifestation of a physical body is "alive" one moment and "dead" the next. Your lack of awareness of the laws of manifestation has kept you from understanding what has occurred. In reality, their energy has merely changed frequencies. It still exists, but it is not vibrating in the human frequency any longer.

In your perceived loss, you grieve the physical human manifestation of someone you love. You miss their human form, and your grief is a very real emotion. Allow yourselves to feel these emotions so that you can come to a new appreciation of your human relationships and the role they play in your lives. Remember, they are not lost to you. You are merely unaware that their energy is still here and available to you to continue in relationship with them. You must lift the veil of separation to understand the means by which that can occur.

To lift the veil you must now match their new vibrational frequency on the other side to be in contact with them. There are many mediums on your planet who have learned how to raise their frequency so they can contact those on the other side of the veil. Through practice and intent, you can learn to be in contact with them. There are also many books available to you on how to contact those who have passed, and We encourage you to follow this path if you so choose. Once you have lifted your vibrations above the veil, your loved ones on the other side will be delighted and enjoy speaking with you. Their love for you goes with them and never fades.

The Law of Attraction

The law of attraction dictates that each thought that you have can manifest into your physical world. That is why it is so important for you to understand the principles of manifestation and to choose your thoughts wisely. The thoughts of those who are unaware of the law of attraction take longer to manifest. This is done for their own protection, as they know not what they are doing and how it will affect them and others. When more time before manifestation is allowed, each person has a short period of time to choose differently. When the thought is repeatedly brought forth, it will eventually manifest and continue to play out until the thought pattern is changed. Simply put, your thoughts are the cause, and your world is the effect or mirror of your thoughts.

For those who are aware of the universal law of attraction or manifestation, the period of time between the thought and manifestation can be more immediate, depending upon your intention and the energy level of your emotions at the time of the thought. This is also done for your benefit, as you can more quickly realize and understand what you have previously sent out into the universe. This allows for easier recognition, association, and learning from what comes back to you.

Your positive energy thoughts can create positive manifestation, or your fearful thoughts can create negative experiences. In some cases, negative thoughts can manifest more quickly because the emotion behind these thoughts is more intense. Be aware of your thoughts and emotional state, and quickly pull back or cancel any negative thoughts so that they are not manifested into your world. Your emotions equate to intent, so how strongly you feel about something dictates how quickly it manifests back to you. Make sure that you infuse all your positive thoughts with much love, positive energy, and gratitude so that these will manifest more quickly for you. The Universal Consciousness is always available to you to assist you in whatever you are doing. Every positive thought, request, or prayer is heard and acted upon.

There Is No Time

In the spirit realm of the Universal Consciousness of God, there is only energy, and as such, there are no limitations associated with a body. You merely think of what it is you want to manifest and it happens immediately. One can manifest unlimited experiences that can all be occurring at the same time. Therefore, there is no time. Time exists only in the physical realm where you have contrasting thoughts. Contrasting thoughts are created out of your egoic mind. Time is a relative term only if you are coming from your egoic thought system within your physical world. The physical realm is the only place where time exists.

Time does not exist in the spiritual realm, where everything is occurring all at once. Every aspect of your life and every potential option that you may choose are all occurring at the same time, within the continuous now. If you were to look at your life as if it were being played out within a computer software game, you would come closer to understanding how the spiritual realm operates. In your software world the programmer of the game would have included all the variable choices and consequences of each choice and further choices and consequences of the original choices and on and on within the game before selling it in the stores. In contrast to the software game, which incorporates only minutes of controlled variations into the software, God instantly created everything in the universe that has ever occurred, could occur now, and could potentially occur in the future, all at the very moment of creation.

This concept may be very difficult for some of you to grasp. When the All that was produced by God was created, the all that was possible was created within the same instant, so that everything that you experience in the now has already occurred. As you live each moment, you are choosing the version of the all that is possible for you at that moment and what you want to create for yourself in the next moment. For most of you, these choices are made subconsciously or by a lack of choice. Either a lack of choice creates the same version of your current experience over and over again or your life becomes affected by the choices of others close to you or a variable combination of both of these. So in this new insight you might now ask yourself, Why would I want to choose to live by the choices of others or by subconscious choices when I don't have to?

Given where most of you are in your ladder back to God, one of the things you may consider is giving all that you do a Divine purpose; in doing so, you ultimately step out of time. That is the significance of learning to intentionally manifest. With all potential choices and outcomes that are available for you to choose at any given time, you will want to choose those that create the type of world that makes you happy. You can either consciously choose what you want to manifest each day or live your life by default choices that may include what has been created by others. New choices are always available to you. You need only to learn how to consciously choose with intent what you want to create in your world. You may also wish to ask the Divine Universe to bring you what is of the highest and best outcome for you.

While there appears to be many problems on your planet, there is really only one. You have forgotten to live your life with love, as one of service to others and your planet.

Chapter 5
The Paradigm Shift

The Need for Change

Some of you are unaware that the need for change on your planet has reached a critical stage and requires Divine intervention to heal. There are those on your planet who are threatening your very existence and who, if left unchecked, will rob you and your offspring of all the natural resources that were so abundantly available to you only a short time ago. Unfortunately, there are many hidden agendas on your planet. There are those who are determined to convert everyone to their religions. There are others who are determined to control all the major resources on your planet. In addition, there are some who are operating from a position of complete and utter greed and don't think about the impact of what they do on your planet. They are destroying your environment, and the health and welfare of their employees, those who use their products, and those who live near their factories.

It is indeed unfortunate, that governments and companies no longer care about what is best for their citizens, natural resources, and planet. Your laws have now been so twisted and misinterpreted as to mandate that the bottom line is more important than what is most beneficial to the good of your social, economic, and planetary systems. There is no longer any accountability for the actions of governments or companies or individuals. Remember that everything you do (the cause) affects someone or something else, and in the end, always you (the effect.)

Although there appear to be many problems on your planet, there is really only one. You have forgotten to live your life with love, as one of service to others and your planet.

Become a nonjudgmental caretaker for your planet and those around you. Take a moment to step back to really see and reflect upon all that you are doing to each other and your planet. With love and compassion in your heart, ask yourself these questions:

When did you stop caring about your brothers and sisters?
When did you stop caring about your planet?
What will it take for you to care again?
What are you lovingly willing to do to change what is occurring?
How can you live in a way that doesn't negatively affect others?
How can you live in a way that doesn't negatively affect your planet?
Are you ready to make a difference now?
Can you make these changes from a place of Love?
Who amongst you will heed the call?

Hearing and acting upon these questions will surely be a stretch for some, but over the course of time, all will come to understand. We have placed many ascended masters and messengers on your planet to assist in your protection and help educate you on these issues. We intercede only when there is grave danger of irreparable damage to your planet or the mass annihilation of its inhabitants. You are on the brink of both. There are so many of you who are unaware of what is actually occurring across your globe. Your lack of independent newspapers and TV and radio stations has caused the information that you hear and read to be skewed to the benefit of the owners. Your TV news prevents you from knowing all that you should know. Journalists are often repressed and threatened when they uncover stories of corruption, greed, decimation, and murder. Out of fear for their own safety, they are no longer driven to expose the truth and inform humanity about what is occurring.

You may choose to take it upon yourselves to stay informed and take action to stop and reverse the effects of the clearing of your rain forests, as they provide you with the very air you breathe. You can choose to stop and reverse the privatization of your freshwater resources before it is too late. You can choose to stop the genetic reengineering of nature and the overprocessing of your food supply before it is too late. You can choose to stop and reverse the effects that strip mining and the use of fossil fuels causes before it is too late. Your chemicals are polluting your food sources and killing you. There are other solutions. Many have invented them, but the greed and corruption of some has caused them to be suppressed and destroyed. Please wake up and stop what is occurring all around you. Make your voice heard around the world.

There are many groups that are leading the way to new legislation and laws to protect your natural resources. Perhaps you will want to assist or make donations so that they can continue this important work. This must be an international endeavor, as many of your precious resources are spread across multiple continents. It is Our hope that enough people, such as yourself, will come forward to ensure governments are held accountable to make the changes necessary for Earth to heal itself. Ask conservation and environmental organizations what you can do to help, and then "just do it," as some on your planet like to say.

Beliefs Required for the Shift

In order to be present in the now and fully participate in the energy and paradigm shifts, you will want to abandon all of your limiting beliefs that no longer serve you. You have many more limiting beliefs than those listed here that have caused you to forget who you are and your purpose for being here. Your individual limiting beliefs also keep you from completing the experiences that you have come here to have. Any belief that keeps you from realizing the truth of who you are and your connectedness additionally blocks all that you could potentially experience. Although your old beliefs served a purpose in your planet's history, you will find with the new energy coming into your planet that they no longer resonate with you, and you may begin replacing them one by one. Replacing old limiting beliefs with your new knowledge of Oneness will spark your internal journey of self-discovery. You are here to experience all that you desire while fulfilling your purpose, and turning inward in your self-discovery is the first step. As you internalize your new beliefs, you will naturally want to be of service to your fellow brothers and sisters.

Truly believing, internalizing, and connecting to Oneness forms the foundation for the beginning of your paradigm shift. To build a new future, you must let go of your past and the beliefs that have perpetuated the current problems. Your current political, socioeconomic, and environmental problems were caused by misinformed generations of self-centeredness and devastation. In remembering, you will understand that you are all a part of everyone and everything, and that what happens to others happens to you. When you take full responsibility for the safekeeping of the planet and your fellow travelers, then you are ready to be a part of this new paradigm shift. Make a conscious choice to shift completely to your new understanding of who you really are and, in that knowing, realize your purpose for being here.

Actions Required for the Shift

There is a new, higher energy coming to your planet. By the end of 2012, this energy will begin to awaken some of you and help your planet reach your next level of evolution. Many of you will experience an internal shift in your spiritual consciousness beginning in 2013. In this next phase of your evolution, children born from now on will be able to live their entire lives knowing their connectedness and purpose for being here. Your lives will be centered on the knowing that you are all connected. And as such, you will make all your decisions based upon the love you have for everyone in your world and what is the highest and best outcome for all involved in those decisions.

As you traverse your spiritual path, your lives will begin to change in many ways. As your medical scientists have recently explained, your species uses only a small fraction of your brains. Your next level of consciousness will manifest through the knowledge gained from your spirit self while connected to the Divine Consciousness. Areas of your brain that have not been used will be activated, and you will begin to understand more about your world and how it operates. All of the knowledge of the Divine Consciousness will be available to those who remember who they are as children of God.

There are also many layers of Divine Consciousness. The heavenly realm through all of its connectedness has order and purpose. This Divine energy ebbs and flows through the thoughts and emotions experienced throughout all of the consciousness of God in the universe. It is important for you to understand that negative thoughts and emotions affect all of the universal Divine energy in a negative way. And positive thoughts of love and joy affect all energy in positive ways. The closer you are to the source of the negative or positive energy, the more you are affected. That is why it is important that you remain in the emotions of peace, love, and Oneness, which are currently the highest emotional vibrational frequencies on your planet.

There are many ways of being in spiritual connectedness. Many can connect to the Divine Consciousness through prayer or meditation or through conversations with those on the other side of the veil. In your next phase of spiritual evolution, you will be able to easily connect with the Universal Consciousness of God. The ongoing elevation of the vibrational energy of your planet allows you to be closer to the frequency of the Divine Consciousness and easily able to connect to your loved ones, angels, and spirit guides.

Changes Occurring in the Shift

Initially the rising energies coming into your planet will cause many to feel out of sorts and not understand what is occurring to them. Tempers may flare and emotions may run high in disproportion to what is actually occurring in relationships, business settings, and governments. Understanding this may occur and being prepared for the changes will allow the discomfort to be minimal. The rising energy can be felt in different ways physically, depending upon your vibrational frequency during the shifts. Some may feel nausea, lightheadedness, or pressure in the head or other similar types of physical discomfort. Initially most will not even be aware of what is occurring to them physically. They will only know that they feel different from how they are used to feeling. Most of these physical symptoms can also be accompanied by a general feeling of being out of sorts. When you surrender and allow the energy of love to encompass you, then you will naturally release your fears and the physical discomfort will vanish.

These new energy levels may also cause you to look more inward at who you are and your purpose for being here. This is the first step in your awakening and remembering. The second step in remembering will occur in how you relate to others. It will begin in your personal relationships, and then shift into your business relationships, then into your governmental relationships. Once you understand your relationships and connectedness, you will be ready to move into the realm of your connectedness to your planet. You will come to understand more intimately how you affect your planet individually and as a species.

Once you are connected with the Universal Divine Consciousness of God, you will cease many of your old patterns of thinking and behaviors on a personal level. You will feel passionate about the health of your planet and want to keep it all in balance. Many of you will begin to experience more enhanced existing relationships. Others will end relationships that no longer make sense to them. Some will seek out others who are at the same level of spiritual consciousness. Do not dwell too much on these changes. Instead, embrace them as part of your new Divine self, as you are a child of God. Thank those who remain in your life, as well as those who move on. Nothing that occurs for you is by accident, and each interaction with someone is an opportunity for spiritual growth. When you follow the voice for truth, the changes you make will be accompanied by joy.

During these periods of new energy shifts, many will feel despair, fear, and other negative energies and emotions. These feelings are there as a means of clearing karmic energy. They can be seen as a catalyst for positive change

or remain as negative energy. When these negative
emotions are left to fester, they become like a cancer,
which can spread like wildfire. When left to run wild with
egoic thoughts, this negative energy can cause physical
manifestations on your planet. Please know that your Earth
physically reacts to the energy of everyone on your planet,
too. It is important to understand this phenomenon and
choose your thoughts wisely. Negative energies will become
more and more physically uncomfortable as the new Earth
energy continues to increase because these lower-frequency
negative emotions are moving farther and farther away from
the new higher vibrations of Earth. To release the physical
symptoms of negative emotions, you will need to shift
your emotions to choose a more positive, higher-frequency
thought.

It would be a good idea to make a conscious decision to
connect with others who are vibrating at the higher levels.
You can actively participate in offering love and prayer for the
healing of all beings and your planet. Participating in national
and international days of prayer can begin a major shift in
raising the energy level of all on your planet. To balance the
Earth energy, consider sending love out from your heart to the
world. Imagine it blanketing the Earth with its healing power
of love. See all men, women, and children surrounded by your
love and basking in its warmth.

Remember that all energy is connected into the Divine All,
including rocks, plants, animals, water life, and people.
Mother Earth simply mirrors back to you that which is going
on within the masses. Whenever you create massive negative
or fearful energy, it can cause the physical manifestation
of hurricanes, tornadoes, earthquakes, and other natural
disasters. This is how Earth rebalances energy between its
crust and the inner core. Additionally, fear can attract these
natural disasters to your physical location as well, so make
a point of staying in the frequency of love wherever you are
located. Also, understand that massive negative energy waves
can also influence world leaders, radicals, terrorists, cities,
towns, families, and you in negative ways.

The goal of the rising energy coming into your planet
is to help as many people as possible be aware of their
connectedness and choose to live in the energies of peace,
love, and Oneness from this point forward. Make it your daily
practice to stay in the emotions of peace, love, and Oneness.
Use meditation, music, and energy clearing to defuse negative
emotions. Listen to calming meditation music as it can
quickly raise your energy frequency above the level where
you feeling uncomfortable. Remember that you can always
speak with the Holy Spirit through your spirit self to ask for
assistance as well.

Through your daily practice of love, compassion, and
harmony with others, you can help them reflect upon
their own thoughts and actions and to then choose a more
loving emotion in which to live. In addition, through these
extensions of love to others, the shift moves more quickly
and pleasantly through the higher energy cycles. And it pays
itself forward to others, who pay it forward in the energy of
love. This way of *being* will ultimately create the beautiful
symphony of love within Oneness.

Active Engagement in the Shift

The higher energies coming into your planet will cause
all living beings on your planet to raise their individual
energetic frequency. While your planet is absorbing the
higher-frequency energy, it is you who will shift in your way
of *being* as this energy naturally raises your frequency. As
mentioned previously, this higher energy is meant to bring
about both physical and spiritual changes within each of you.
These new evolutional physical changes will eventually allow
each person to actively and consciously have access to and
engage in the Universal Divine Consciousness.

One of the things you can do to benefit your body is to eat
healthy, organic, raw, and unprocessed foods. The foods
found in your supermarkets today are overly processed and
are of little value to you nutritionally. And much of your
food supply has poisonous pesticides in it as well. For those
eating poor diets, the new energy will exacerbate any health

issues you currently have. Changing your eating habits to include eating mostly raw, organic fruits and vegetables will benefit you in many ways. A raw diet will also assist your body with the changes that will occur as a result of the higher energy coming into your planet. A regular routine of physical exercise will assist you as well. Taking a daily brisk walk for twenty to thirty minutes will also allow your physical energy to synchronize with the new energy levels of Earth. Your walk will help dissolve feelings of discord or uneasiness caused by the imbalance between your energy frequency and that of Earth.

During the initial stages of these changes, there may be physical feelings of discomfort as mentioned previously. Remember to stay diligent to consciously remain in the higher emotional frequencies. If you are already living in the higher frequencies, you will feel less discomfort as the new energy is raised to the next level. The people who will have the most difficult time during these periods are those who are living and experiencing their emotions in the lower egoic emotional frequencies. Each of your emotions vibrates at a different frequency. The positive emotions of peace, love, joy, and Oneness vibrate at a very high level. The negative emotions of shame, guilt, apathy, grief, fear, desire, anger, and pride vibrate from a very low-frequency level and will cause you real physical discomfort.

As previously mentioned, each of your energies affects all those around you and ultimately the universe as a whole. Raising your vibrations begins with a change in how you view the world around you. Change your view and you change your reality.

Take a moment to understand the Map of Consciousness below that was Divinely inspired through David Hawkins. It is a good representation of the types and levels of emotions and their associated vibrational frequencies. It would be good to know and understand this chart in detail so that you can realize how your emotions affect everything and everyone around you. Do not take this lightly, as it is a law of universal truth, whether you believe it to be so or not.

Map of Consciousness					
God-View	Life-View	Level	Log	Emotion	Process
Self	Is	Enlightenment	700-1000	Ineffable	Pure Consciousness
All Being	Perfect	Peace	600	Bliss	Illumination
One	Complete	Joy	540	Serenity	Transfiguration
Loving	Benign	Love	500	Reverence	Revalation
Wise	Meaningful	Reason	400	Understanding	Abstraction
Merciful	Harmonious	Acceptance	350	Forgiveness	Transcendence
Inspiring	Hopeful	Willingness	310	Oprimiam	Intention
Enabling	Satisfactory	Neutrality	250	Trust	Release
Permitting	Feasible	Courage	200	Affirmation	Empowerment
Indifferent	Demanding	Pride	175	Scorn	Inflation
Vengeful	Antagonistic	Anger	150	Hate	Agression
Denying	Disappointing	Desire	125	Craving	Enslavement
Punitive	Frightening	Fear	100	Anxiety	Withdrawal
Disdainful	Tragic	Grief	75	Regret	Despondent
Condenming	Hopeless	Apathy	50	Despair	Abdication
Vindictive	Evil	Guilt	30	Blame	Destruction
Despising	Miserable	Shame	20	Humiliation	Elimination
	The Final Doorway to Enlightenment / Nonduality				
	The Beginning of the Nonlinear Realm				
	The Beiginning of Integrity				

David Hawkins Map of Consciousness

Take a look at the chart and find the feeling of guilt, which would be vibrating at the level of thirty, and see that someone at this level would feel blame, destruction, evil, and vindictiveness toward others. These are destructive behavioral processes and would negatively affect your relationships if acted upon or left to fester. In contrast, if you are at the level of love, which is five hundred, then you will feel reverence for those around you, and you will lovingly enjoy your relationships more fully.

While you reflect on this list of emotions, also remember that all emotions, thoughts, words, and actions that you originate will cause you to have similar events reflected to you as karma at some future time. At its worst, if left unchecked, guilt can cause you to have circular relationships that bring about further guilt, blame, and vindictiveness until you decide to choose another emotion to engage. Take the time each day to notice your feelings and see where you are vibrating and compare it with where you would like to be. Determine to make a conscious choice to shift how you wish to feel up into a higher vibrational level. Choose to focus on the blessings in your life and send out love to those around you, and your life will be enhanced in many ways.

Understanding What Is Truly Important

This book is about empowerment and taking full responsibility for who you are as a child of God. It is about taking action. It is also intended to assist you in protecting your future, as well as the future of your children and their children. It is through your choice to take positive, loving, and peaceful actions that change can occur. To date many of you have been called to come forward to take up this mantle, but many have yet to step forward to bring about the changes that are so desperately needed now. It is going to take all of you to become dedicated to the cause of healing your planet to bring about these changes. Please consider stepping forward to be counted!

Your Divinely guided purpose and actions can be the impetus for important changes that can bring peace to your planet for thousands of years. Turn inward to discover your purpose, as each individual has a purpose that is unique to him or her. This is truly an important period for your planet. Your role in this significant evolutionary period was predetermined before you arrived here. Each person on your planet today is here because he or she wanted to assist in bringing about these changes. Unfortunately, there are many who are still asleep and unaware of their purpose. If you haven't already, take the time now to remember your purpose and begin to live it fully.

Some of you may experience fear around the thought that your purpose might be different from what you are currently living today. That is a normal emotion and part of the process in your awakening. For some of you, change will be required to fulfill your purpose. If that is the case, remember that you are never alone in your journey and that We are here to assist you. You need merely ask for our help and it will be so. Once you are living your true purpose, it will make your heart sing with joy and happiness. It is through living your life's purpose that you will know true joy, peace, and love.

It is time to take up your purpose and proceed forward in your life's mission. You may require training to learn your new purpose. Seek out those who are already in your new field. They can help you learn what you need to know. Connect to the Universal Consciousness so you can become Divinely guided each day. Your daily directions can become your guiding light on your path of ascension and help you best assist others on their path as well.

Shifting Social Mores

In order for your planet to heal, there needs to be a major shift in social beliefs and order. Your social mores vary from location to location and country to country. There is nothing wrong with differences, as long as they are coming from a place of love. Some of your current social mores are based upon commercialism and obtaining goods to "make you happy." Please know that there is nothing outside of you that can make you happy. Happiness can come only from living your life from love and purpose. Do not let the corporations of the world dictate to you what can make you happy. Go within to seek the love that is yours, and in remembering, you will find your happiness.

There are a few enlightened leaders who are standing up for what is right for everyone. Others are living with an attitude of "each man for himself" and have closed their eyes to the needs of others. In the new energy, this type of selfishness will eventually fade, and people will naturally want to reconnect in unity. There are many adjustments that can be made to change what is occurring on your planet. It will entail making the changes on a personal level first, then moving your focus to a local, national, and global scale. These can occur rather rapidly once you know and understand your role in the world today. Remember that you are all connected and that what you do for another is what you ultimately do for yourself. Reach out to those who are in need and help them, as whatever you do for the least of them, you are doing for yourself and God.

Begin your new life by speaking the truth in every moment, as it is from truth that you will come to really know the Divine Consciousness. Do not make up stories about what you perceive, but merely observe without judgment and allow others to live as who they are at each moment. Each moment is an opportunity for you to understand what you have come here to experience, both for yourself as well as for the others you will encounter along the way. Choose to abandon the need to fit in, as you already do. You are all connected, and need only to remember the truth of your Oneness. Life is not about looking good to others. It is about living your life's purpose through love, peace, joy, and Oneness. It is seeing and recognizing the soul of another first in all your interactions that leads to the peace of God. Connect soul to soul in your communications with others telepathically first, then proceed in your encounter from that place of *being*. You need merely think that is what you'd like to do and it will occur. When you do this, you will find the positive changes in your interactions amazing.

Choose to abandon the need to possess things, as they do not define you. See objects as they truly are, tools to accomplish a purpose. "If only I had this or that, I would be happy" appears to be the way some on your planet live each day. Happiness doesn't come from outside of you. It can only be found from within. Although there is nothing wrong with possessing things, it is the purpose you give them that defines the outcome of their use. What are you using them for? Are you sharing what you have? Have you given them a Divine purpose? It is through living your life from within the emotions of love, peace, joy, and Oneness that you attain happiness. All else is an illusion.

Live life simply so that all may simply live. There are enough resources on your planet for all of your fellow brothers and sisters. You are each caregivers of your planet and all that inhabit it. Take only what you need and replace what you take. Recycle everything. Give back to your planet so that it may continue to provide for future generations. Stop using your scarce resources. Research and understand how industries affect your environment. Choose to stop those practices that cause pollution and devastation to your environment. Provide your brothers and sisters with the education, knowledge, and resources needed to help them become self-sustaining. Make it your conscious choice to live your life knowing that you are here to assist in healing your planet and helping others to awaken. This new order will be brought about through your new level of spiritual evolution and consciousness.

Choose to stop the deforestation of your rain forests. Help raise your planet's consciousness toward these issues. These trees provide you the oxygen you breathe, and without them, you will not survive as a species. These trees take hundreds of years to grow to a size that has any effect upon your planet. Every year that you cut these trees down is a year you are subtracting from your children's lives. You cannot recover in time the trees you are currently cutting to support all who are alive on your planet today, let alone the increasing populations of tomorrow. If change isn't immediate, the effect is going to be devastating. Choose to stop these catastrophic practices immediately for your planet's future. Contact your elected officials to let them know that these practices can no longer be tolerated. Consider boycotting the companies funding these practices.

Choose to stop the use of fossil fuels, coal, and strip mining for generating power. There are other, more sustainable means by which to provide energy to your planet. Support your inventors, embrace their causes, and protect them from those who want to maintain the status quo. After you have done that, you can incorporate the new technologies into your daily lives. Choose to manifest and live the dream of having a world where everyone nurtures your planet and all the beings that share it with you. Show the world that by loving Mother Earth, she will be able to provide all that you need.

Choose to abandon genetic reengineering of life. It is already perfect and how it was intended. All resources on your planet are a gift to you for safekeeping. Use them, but do not use them up or abuse them. Life is exactly as God intended. You will find that the foods made from these plants will eventually lead to disease and an early death for many. Just because you can do it does not mean that you should choose to do so.

Once your planet is back in balance, all of you will be able to more fully enjoy all that is available to you. Your lives will change in many positive ways. Your focus will be on the quality of your lives and not on consumerism. The joy that is in store for you as you begin to pursue what is truly important in your lives is amazing. The fifth dimension will bring with it many new gifts each of you will be able to incorporate into your lives. It will be through these gifts that you can find more connectedness and love in all your relationships. What a wondrous time of hope and change is upon you now.

In order to begin the process of accepting your new way of being, you must understand how you have showed up on this planet so far in this lifetime.

Chapter 6
Embracing Change

Embracing Change

Each and every one of you on your planet today is here at this time to help facilitate ushering in the new world order. This new world order is unlike any that has been possible for many millennia. You are moving from a third-, to a fourth-, and then a fifth-dimensional world. There is much to learn so that you can understand what this means in terms of your daily lives and how you may prepare for these changes. Most on your planet will be oblivious to these changes and will know only that they feel different from last year, although they won't be aware of why. They will continue to act, speak, and do as they have up until now, staying completely disconnected to all that is their birthright. As the energy continues to rise, they will eventually begin to feel more and more physical discomfort and their lives will have more and more drama. This continued drama will cause them to step back to look at their lives. It is when they turn inward to reflect on how they are living that they will begin to understand that there has to be another way of being. Those who seek a better way to live their lives will begin to reflect the love, joy, and happiness of an intentional spiritual life. You will also begin to find that much is available to assist you in your ascension process.

This book is the primer to my next book of more extensive teachings on how you may choose to *be* in Oneness. My next book will provide you with suggestions for how you may choose to live your daily lives and will include a daily lesson workbook on how you may practice *being* in Oneness. Please notice my wording that these teachings and workbook lessons will be suggestions on how to live and not rules that must be followed. They will be provided to you as a means to show you what has worked well for other societies that have been living in Oneness for thousands of years.

Make it your daily practice to understand what is occurring to you and for you as you move forward into these new dimensions. You must prepare yourselves for these energy events coming to your planet if you wish to take advantage of the gifts available to you within each of these new dimensions. As you progress in your spiritual growth, new gifts will be given to you to assist you in your further ascension.

There are many beliefs that you may wish to discard as you embrace remembering who you are as a child of God. Consider releasing those that no longer serve you, and embrace these new beliefs. You will also be guided to adopt new practices that can assist you with the changes that will be occurring to your planet, its energy field, and your spirit self, body, and DNA. These new ways of being will assist you in learning all that is available to you in the new fourth dimension that you will soon be entering. Your planet will migrate from your third-dimensional world into a fourth- and then onto a fifth-dimensional realm. The time frame of these shifts is not set in stone and can change depending upon how quickly or slowly your planet adapts and adopts the new life principles that will be sent to guide you. Nevertheless, ready or not: changes are coming.

This may not be an easy path for some of you. Some will fight this new way of being with all of their might, money, and influence, but to no avail. Eventually the enlightened ones who have accepted the responsibility to lead this movement to the fourth and fifth dimensions will prevail, and your planet will be blessed with thousands of years of peace, prosperity, joy, and happiness as a result. This is not a short-term experience, but a long-term commitment of the enlightened to ensure that what has been intended for humankind is manifested for all on your planet. Eventually even those who have steadfastly fought change will come to understand the joys of living through love and will begin to embrace the new world order.

In order to begin the process of accepting your new way of being, you must understand how you have showed up on this planet so far in this lifetime. It is important that you truly understand you are a child of God. You are love, and as such, you need to live your daily lives from your heart and not your egos. You must see each person you come into contact with as a continuation of yourself and your brother/sister in God's Sonship.

Viewing each person you see as love, no matter what their thoughts, words, or actions show you, is the key to your shift in consciousness. They are made of Divine energy and merely need to awaken to that knowledge. With this Divine shift in energy also comes your option to forgive all transgressions your ego perceives have been committed against you in this lifetime. In reality, no one has ever harmed you in any way. Some of you will take a stance of being indignant to my last comment, and I would ask that you allow me to explain. Because you are a spirit manifesting in a body, no one could possibly harm you, nor can you harm another. You are God's energy, and as such, are indestructible and will remain Divine energy into eternity. Your human ego merely believes it has been harmed because it has forgotten its origin.

Although the egoic thought system can and does choose to act in very negative ways, no one is truly harmed. Yes, there is pain, injury, and a loss of physical manifestation (life) and this appears real in your lower dimensions, but your spirit self does not experience this. It merely moves back into the higher realms of Divinity and continues to experience at that level. Remember, the God energy that you are made of makes each of you incapable of anything but love. Your spirit self feels nothing but love. To understand this you must look beyond what your earthly eyes and ego sees. Your ego only sees the physical body of another. Release your ego so that you can see the soul/spirit within them. Close your eyes and imagine the radiant spirit that is the core of each and every person. That is what is real. When you recognize others as they truly are, you should be able to see that each living being has an energy field or aura around it. This aura is what is real, true, and who you really are, not the physical body that your eyes see. Your physical body is merely a cloak that you are wearing for this lifetime and will be laid aside once it has been used, worn, and served the purpose you have given it in this lifetime. Your cloak merely allows you to experience this physical lifetime using your physical senses along with your Divine essence. As such, it is a means by which you can grow spiritually. It is through your experiences with others that you can *be* the Love that is God for all those who share the physical plane with you. Your purpose is to become the highest expression of God's love within each relationship that shows up to you in this incarnation. It is through these loving experiences that you ascend into the higher dimensions of physical manifestation.

Recognizing Your Purpose for Being Here

You have come to Earth at this time to assist your planet in rising from a third- to a fifth-dimensional world. Your purpose here is closely aligned with this shift in both the physical and metaphysical realms. This rise in dimensions has sweeping ramifications for your planet and how you view your world today. Most of you have come down to this planet now to assist others in remembering who they are as children of God and to awaken them to fulfill their purposes during this very important time for all of you. Also, know that your purpose may change as your path leads you into a new or different aspect of your purpose.

Once you have remembered who you are as a child of God, your next step is to release your egos so that you may fully step into your spirit self. Releasing your ego is not an easy task and will require many changes to your belief systems. During this process, you will begin to remember your purpose for being here at this time. Once you have opened yourself fully to the truth of your existence, you will be ready to begin working toward releasing your egoic thought system. As part of your learning process, make sure you check in daily with your spirit guide so that you can be gently guided in what to do and say in your new way of *being*.

Releasing your ego will require daily learning and practices such as those put forward in my previous teachings from *A*

Course in Miracles. Choose to study and understand these teachings so that you may be able to fully comprehend the effect of the egoic thought system on your daily lives. Only after understanding and recognizing how the egoic thought system works will you be able to step away from the ego and into the light of Oneness.

The process of understanding your ego and releasing its control over you cannot be circumvented, as it is a prerequisite to advancing spiritually. The first step in this process is to recognize your ego at work in your daily lives. From there you need to step back to see what is real and then choose to experience living through your spirit self instead. For those who resist this process, the ego will persist in throwing roadblocks in the way to prevent your advancement. Know that your ego will also bring up much fear for you during this process. The fear is meant to block your acceptance of your truth and advancement in your knowing who you are as a child of God.

Your ego has many, many fears but ultimately believes that once you are enlightened, you will have no further use for it. The ego believes that you cannot live without it and that you will die if it is not fully engaged. Nothing is further from the truth. In reality, it will be at this point that you are ready to begin living as you were truly intended to on this planet. Remember that you are not a body with a soul. You are a soul incarnated into a physical body.

To clear these fears, you must first acknowledge them, understand that they are erroneous beliefs, and then release them, as they no longer serve you. Ask your spirit self to show you why you are feeling fear. Once you have that answer, then ask yourself, "What can I learn from this?" Then ask your spirit self to release this fear to God for cleansing and transmutation. The same fear may come up multiple times, as it may have come about from multiple encounters. Examine it as explained above and release it again. You will need to repeat this process for each fear that presents itself to you. Once you have released your most prominent fears, you will begin to feel the peace that that has been missing from your life, and you will experience more joy.

Releasing the egoic thought system can take a long time for many of you, as it will require that you completely tear down and then rebuild a new foundation of learning how to *be* and interact with others. What your egos have taught you does not serve you any longer and keeps you from all that is your birthright. Invite the Holy Spirit to be with you in all that you do each day, and your life will begin to be glorious in every way. In your yearning to find what is lacking in your lives, each of you in reality misses the Love of God you experienced in the Universal Oneness before coming down here. Once the ego has been released, you will have full access to fully feel this Love once again. You will merely need to think about God's Love to be blanketed in it once again.

Those Who Have Begun Their Enlightenment

Some of you reading this book have already begun your spiritual enlightenment process. You know who you are as children of God and how to show up in your daily lives with others. To those I say, "Thank you" and ask that you continue on your path, as this is only the first step in your path of who you can become in this lifetime and at this special time. As part of your continued growth, you will need to connect with the Holy Spirit through your spirit self so that you may come to know your detailed purpose and receive your daily spiritual guidance. This is most often done through daily morning and evening meditations. A daily practice of clearing and cleansing your spiritual energy chakras should become a part of these daily meditations as well. Once you know your purpose, it is time for taking action to live your purpose.

As you continue to advance on your road to enlightenment, you may feel you no longer require daily meditations to receive your spiritual messages, as answers will occur as any question arises in your mind from minute to minute. I would ask that you continue in this daily meditation practice, as it is how the masters have become masters. It is when you assume that you no longer need assistance in your process of enlightenment that you are really in the most need of it. Arrogance is the ego pretending to be the spirit self.

Whenever you are confronted with a situation where your egoic thought system reacts instead of your spirit self, this is a sign that your ego has begun to intrude into your thoughts and dilute the purity of your messages. You can recognize these times by monitoring your emotions. If you are feeling any emotions other than love, joy, and happiness, then your ego is actively at work in your life. As your messages now occur more frequently throughout your day, please remember that your spiritual energy chakras may require additional cleansing and clearing after any egoic episodes in your day so that your messages remain pure and of Divine origin.

Messages received after a cleansing and meditation will usually have the highest likelihood of Divine origin. You may wish to ask your spirit self to ensure that only those messages of Divine origin come to you. Let your emotions be your guide when interpreting your messages. If you feel the least bit uneasy after a message, then consider a chakra cleansing and clearing and ask for Divine guidance again afterward. If you feel good about a message, then it was probably from a Divine origin. If you are uneasy or unsure about the message, then it is very likely from the ego. Let your emotions be your gauge. Remember, it is a process of growth and learning to stay in the vortex of love. When you feel that you have drifted from the peace of God, then you know what to do to bring yourself back into alignment with the Universal Divine.

It is very important that you also understand that during this special time on your planet, each of you has the opportunity to advance spiritually at a very fast rate. If you so choose, you can advance within this current lifetime what would normally take you many lifetimes to accomplish. You merely need to step into the light of your spirit self and ask to know what else you can do to advance spiritually. You will then be guided toward the next step on your personal ascension path. As always, there is never a need to do anything, as you are all given free will and choice in everything that you do. You are all loved as you are and where you are in your path, so do what resonates in your soul.

The Energy Coming Into Your Planet

The current energy shift coming into your planet now will serve to catapult your planet into the fourth dimension. This energy will continue for many years and will fully transition you from the fourth into the fifth dimension as you continue to evolve. The energy that has been coming into your planet for some time now is to prepare you for the physical changes that must occur within each person before your transition to the next dimension. Each person will be made ready to receive the higher vibrational frequencies of the fourth and then fifth dimensions. All living beings on your planet will complete these physical changes whether or not they are aware of what is occurring or believe in it.

The changes that have already begun are occurring slowly, and the majority of those on your planet are completely unaware of them. Many of you may feel some discomfort and tingling in those areas of your body where these changes are activated. Depending upon your spiritual advancement, the physical and spiritual changes being made to and around your body that will continue to occur over several years include the following:

- Your dormant DNA strands will again be activated and over time eventually increase from two to twelve strands.

- Your spiritual and body energy and meridian centers will be fully activated and expanded.

- Your organs will increase in size to accommodate the increased frequencies and allow for improved bodily functions.

- Dormant organs and portions of other organs will be activated and grow to their beneficial size to help the body perform within these higher-frequency functions.

- The energy coming into the planet will allow you to more easily recognize, learn from, and release past energy distortions and negative karma from this and previous lives.

Physical Changes Bring New Abilities

The new physical changes to your bodies will not only allow you to function at a higher frequency, but will allow other benefits as well. These gifts will be awakened in you as you grow spiritually and can accept the responsibility that goes with each gift. The benefits that may be available as you spiritually advance include the following:

- The merging of your spirit self with your body.

- The ability to heal yourself and others through the power of intent.

- A much longer life span for those who embrace healthful eating and lifestyle practices.

- The ability to communicate telepathically with others in a mind-to-mind communication. (This may occur over short or long distances.)

- The ability to communicate with those who have passed.

- The ability to intentionally manifest your thoughts into reality.

- The ability to change weather patterns through group prayer and intent.

- The ability to understand and speak languages you have not known in the past.

- The ability to bring into your present awareness lessons learned from your past and future lives.

- The ability to bring past and future experiences into your experience of now.

- Time as you know it will expand to multiple dimensions. There are twelve dimensions of time, only three of which you are now aware (past, present, and future).

Other Earth Changes

Other changes to your planet that your scientists have begun
to document include a shifting of the axis of your planet.
It has already shifted slightly and will continue to change
over time. There is nothing to be concerned about with
these changes, as they allow Earth and your solar system to
align more precisely with the center of the Milky Way. This
new alignment also allows the higher realms of spiritual
dimensions to flow more freely to your planet and assist
you in your purpose for being here. Your scientists will
soon begin to notice that your planet's orbit around the sun
is shifting as well. This will also occur as a result of your
solar system realigning with the center of the Milky Way.
Because of the expansion of the universe, your planet will
begin to experience a slow change in its pattern of rotation
around the sun, as well as an increase in the speed of the daily
rotation on its axis. The effects of these slight shifts will be
realized through changes to your weather patterns and your
current structure of time. These new patterns of rotation will
eventually cause your calendar year to elongate and your days
to shorten.

Your weather patterns will also slowly change from what you
are experiencing now. Depending upon where you are located
on your planet in relation to your new slightly shifted North
and South Poles, your weather patterns will shift accordingly.
Again, this is all a matter of degrees and is not something
that should elicit any fear or concern. Since your days will
eventually be shorter, the growth cycles for your crops and
plants will change slightly as well. The germination and
growing cycles will take longer, much as they are today for
those areas on your planet where daylight is limited during
certain periods of the year. Remember that all of life adjusts
as change presents itself, much as man has done throughout
your history of time.

The Balancing of Earth

The awakening of your planet is at hand, and there is much
that will be occurring over the next twenty-five years. Your

ascension does not stop there and continues for hundreds of years. There has been and will continue to be super-storms and natural disasters that will happen as an outcome of balancing Earth's inner core with the new energy coming into your planet. The hurricanes, tornadoes, earthquakes, and other natural disasters serve to release trapped energy held within the power nodes of your planet. These releases of old energy and the accepting of the new energy allow your planet to ascend to its next dimensional level. As with each of you, your planet will ascend with similar pains of change, and the greater good of all will be served in the process.

The balancing adjustments that have been occurring and will continue to occur over these years will circumvent any global cataclysmic events that have occurred previously in your Earth history. We rarely intervene in planetary shifts, but without these incremental adjustments that have been and will continue to be orchestrated on your behalf, your planet would experience major events that could eradicate most of life there. These incremental events are meant to balance the new energy of your planet in its shift to higher dimensions and within its new positioning in your Milky Way in a more gentle way.

It is important to understand that these natural disasters are an important balancing aspect of your ascension and that without them, it could not occur. It should also be known that the energy produced in these storms has properties that can react to energies produced by humans in large areas of populations. Storms and other natural disasters are balancing the releases of energy. These energies are attracted to lower vibrational energy. Super-hurricanes act as mechanisms to supercharge the oceans with the new energies. They are intended to stay out at sea. If a large number of people react within the lower frequencies of fear to these storms, they can ultimately attract the storms to them. Know these things about energy and understand them so that you can play your part in keeping your personal energy in the higher frequency of love so as to allow these storms to run their natural course of travel.

Living in the frequency of love will greatly assist in keeping these storms from affecting life. Please do not let your media traumatize you with their predictions, drama, and sensationalism. The fear these programs generate does not serve you. Prepare for the storms and take precautions, but do not fall prey to the fear. Please be aware that praying to keep the storms away is also coming from fear and should be avoided. If you wish to do something, then sit in meditation and surround the storm with a blanket of love. Dissolve your fear and lovingly ask the Holy Spirit to provide for the highest and best outcome for the storm.

Balancing the energy of your planet is a natural process and will continue into infinity. Your own energy is always balancing within the energy of the All. It is affected by the energy of those around you. Additionally, your energy affects all that is around you. Your natural way of being is in the frequency of love. Engage your life from love and all will be as it should be for you and your planet.

Time in Your New World

Your relationship with time will change significantly in your new world dimensions. As your planet shifts on its axis and travels farther from the sun, it will slightly change your pattern of days, weeks, months, and years. The change will not occur all at once, so there will need to be periods of recalculation and recalibration of your measurement of time as your solar system and planet shift into their new position within the Milky Way. Many scientists will help recalculate and incorporate these changes to create new days, weeks, months, and years into your new reality of time. How you view your new time can be perceived as a slight variation to what is currently considered standard, or it can be viewed as an opportunity to rethink how you view what is truly important in your lives.

You are current enslaved to time. Remember that I have mentioned earlier that living simple lives allows for joy, peace, and harmony to abound. With these shifts in time, many may want to more tightly control your days, weeks, and months of the year. Many governments and corporations will insist that you commit a higher percentage of each day to work rather than to what is truly important in your lives. I would ask that you consider choosing to resist these types of changes with all the power within you. As you consider these changes, let your hearts open up and your voices be heard. Do not further enslave yourselves to changes that are clearly not in your best interest. Life is meant to *be* experienced without the shackles of tightly monitored, daily work routines. At the end of the day, your work provides you nothing more than a roof over your head and food for your stomachs.

Your purpose here is to experience life through your relationships with others, and that should be your primary focus of each day. Climbing the corporate ladder and obtaining all the objects that make you believe you have self-worth are what keeps you from this purpose. Life is for love, joy, excitement, and laughter. Keep that in your focus as you contemplate your new world in the near future. Make sure your voices are heard while thoughts and ideas float around you about these changes. Creating balance in your daily lives is what brings you joy. Cherish this and the people in your lives, and you will all reap the benefits that life can provide you. You are meant to cheerfully enjoy your physical manifestation in this lifetime.

Prior to coming down to Earth, each person worked with their spirit guides to choose the experiences they wished to accomplish in this lifetime. In planning your life, you made agreements with those who would become your parents, birth families, and the key people who would come into your life.

Chapter 7
Your Purpose

Your Purpose for Being Here

One of the most challenging aspects of understanding your spirituality is gaining the knowledge of your purpose for being here. Some of you do not currently know your purpose for being here at this time. Many ask to know but have yet to hear their responses. They may have blocked the information coming to them or aren't vibrating at the energy of love, which is necessary to hear their messages. Moreover, there are those whose egos don't accept the answer, and then they may begin to think the information is incorrect or disregard the response. To hear your purpose, begin by sitting in the quiet of meditation, without thoughts, then ask the question and listen for the response. If you are practiced at meditation, your answer should come fairly quickly. But if you are new to meditation, you may need to practice it for a while to become adept at raising your vibrations to the level that you can hear your spirit guides or angels.

Before coming down to Earth, each person worked with their spirit guides to choose the experiences they wished to accomplish in this lifetime. In planning your life, you made agreements with those who would become your parents, birth families, and the key people who would come into your life. You also made arrangements with others to mutually assist each other in your journeys. These planned experiences and your chosen relationships are meant to provide learning and spiritual advancement during each lifetime. Now that you know this, you can understand that each person who is put into your path is there to provide you with valuable learning and understanding for your spiritual path. Although your purpose may be different at the form level, the true underlying purpose for everyone in the physical realm is to become a vortex for love for all who come into your life. With this new information, you can understand these learning experiences in a new light and better see how they may play out for you moving forward. When you resist or are unaware of what roles these opportunities are offering you, there is a higher potential for drama and discord in these experiences.

You can better understand these experiences when you are able to step back and ask the Holy Spirit to show you what you are to learn from them. If you really listen within the quiet of meditation, your answer will come, and you will then understand the true role you are to play in this event. Keep in mind that all experiences you have are ultimately meant as a means for you to show up as the highest manifestation of love that you are able to present at that moment toward another. You will want to fully understand the role you were destined to play in each event, as it is an experience for each person involved. What is best for you is really what is best for all involved.

Your purpose at any given time may be different from what it was one year ago or even one week ago. As you learn and mature spiritually, your life also changes in how it can play out moving forward. You have changed, so therefore, your outcome has shifted you from where you were previously as well. Life will play out as an ebb and flow of new energy as possibilities are presented to you as an outcome of your new personal growth. You always have the opportunity to continue to grow spiritually even after you have accomplished all that you intended in this lifetime.

Although your core purpose may change at the form level, it will always remain a part of helping others to remember who they are. That is why it is important to continue to meditate daily and listen to your spiritual guides to learn what direction has the highest and best potential outcome for you and others as you move forward in your daily life. Do not fall prey to comparing your purpose to that of others, as that is an egoic response. Your purpose is that which causes you to grow spiritually at this time. Rest assured that you have probably lived many lifetimes of very different purposes and perhaps have already completed that to which you are now comparing yourself.

The information you receive from your spirit guides can sometimes appear to be confusing, and you may even question its authenticity. Check in to clarify any messages that come to you. Know that all Divine messages are loving, nurturing, and informational. Messages from your ego are typically egotistical, judgmental, demanding, or self-serving. If you feel unsure of your messages, your ego may have inserted itself and made you think it is incorrect—or it can indeed be incorrect. Check in with your emotions to make sure that you have made a clear connection to spirit, and that you are truly hearing what is being presented. Don't be hard on yourself if you have a difficult time hearing your messages. Merely take a break, clear your energy chakras, raise your vibrations to love, and try again. When you are truly listening and having no other thoughts, you are ready to hear your guided messages. If you make a mistake, simply ask the Holy Spirit to correct it and try again.

Your Purpose in Oneness

During this time in your history, people are awakening after a very long slumber to remember who they are and what their role is in this great event. As mentioned earlier, you are all here now to step into your purpose and assist the world in awakening. Knowing your purpose is one of the most difficult steps in your enlightenment. Many of you are remotely aware of what your purpose might be. However, some of you may have allowed your egos to talk you out of it for various reasons. Your purpose is what makes your heart sing and brings you great joy. If you don't know or aren't sure of your purpose, keep asking yourself, "What is my purpose?" And if you listen with love in your heart, you will hear the answer from your spirit self, angels, or spirit guide.

Some of you know your purpose and are doing what you are intended to do. Others of you may find that a career change is required for you to step into your power. For those of you who are already working in your intended field, your new focus may be to more fully perform your job as a vortex for love while doing what is best for your customers, employees, mankind, and your planet. Some of you may choose to make changes to how governments and businesses operate as your purpose. In doing this purpose you will allow your planet to come back into balance with the universe. Although profits will remain a primary focus for your near future, know that irresponsibility and greed will not survive in the new world order.

For those of you who will be changing careers, a transition period may be required to become proficient in your new field of work. Some of you may wonder how this could possibly occur while maintaining income to support yourself and your families. I would answer by saying that you will be guided to take action when the timing is right for you. This action may include new training or education to prepare for your new field of work. You will need to be aware and listen to your spirit self to hear these messages, so sitting in the quiet of love in your daily meditations will be very important to you moving forward. If you should miss an opportunity that was presented to you, do not fear. As you become more fully attuned to your spirit self and your messages, you will be presented with additional events that can propel you into your intended field of work.

Ignoring Divine Messages

Divine messages are constantly coming to each being living in the physical realm. In the third dimension, many are still unaware they are being sent guiding messages, and they live their lives by default through their egos. Although there can be many good outcomes when living through your egoic thought system, it is difficult to attain the joy that is your inheritance. Performing tasks that are a part of your soul purpose brings you great joy and a sense of accomplishment that simply cannot be attained from egoic actions. There is happiness in living your life knowing that your new priorities are what are best for you and everyone in your life. There is also a greater peace for those who are living their purpose.

For those who know their purpose but are not living it, eventually your life will begin to reflect pain and drama, as you are not in harmony with the Divine Universe. This pain and drama will eventually become too great and motivate you to begin to look again at what you are doing and how best to move forward. Your spirit guides are there to assist you with making the highest and best choices for you in your daily living, thereby allowing you to avoid negative outcomes. They are connected to the Universal Divine Knowledge and already know the potential outcomes to the thoughts, words, and deeds you may be considering. When asked, they can provide you with what you could be doing on a daily basis and keep you moving in the direction in which you are destined as part of your purpose. The outcomes they can provide you will make your path so much easier than living without guidance. As always, you have a free will to choose what path you wish to take in each moment of each day and that is perfect for you.

If you choose to ignore your messages from your spirit guides, there is nothing wrong with that. However, if you have been on your spiritual path and enjoy the benefits of living purposefully, you may soon feel the loss of the peace you attained through receiving daily guidance. The loss of the peace and joy from not doing what you came down here to do can feel quite disconcerting. You may not want to sit too long within this feeling of lack of peace, as coming from lack will ensure that it continues. Your loss of peace is not an indication of being bad or wrong, but simply indicates that you are listening to the wrong voice. Merely recognize your mistake and choose the voice of God again.

If you choose to continue to ignore your messages, you may begin to feel that your life has become aimless and unfulfilling. If these feelings are left to fester, you may start to spiral down into the lower emotional feelings and have self-doubts. You also may begin to have experiences that were not intended for you, which can lead you to a life lived by default or from others' choices. It is at this point that you will need Us the most, and We hope that you can remember to sit in the peace of meditation and call upon Us once again to assist you. It is always a matter of choice for each person. You all have free will in deciding what to choose in every moment of each day. It is our hope that your path is full of peace, love, joy, and Oneness so that you may know how much you are truly loved.

Remember to ask for our assistance, and We will be there for you at every turn. Whatever We may do to assist you brings us our greatest joy. We are only a thought away.

Helping Others to Know Their Purpose

Most of you on Earth today are here to assist others in remembering who they are as children of God. This very special time for your planet has called for many souls to come forward to physically manifest. It is important that all your brothers and sisters awaken so that they may remember and embrace all that they are as children of God. There is much to be accomplished to move your planet toward living in the fifth dimension. You are here to create a world that can embrace your new humanity, and this requires many changes. These changes will eventually manifest for each of you both internally and externally in how you live your lives.

Helping others know their purpose will be a challenge for many of you. There are so many who are unaware and don't have the slightest inkling that they have a purpose to perform while living here on this planet. It may be frustrating to you at first as you observe those who could benefit from knowing who they are and their purpose for being here. You may be inclined to want to convince them that they need this information and that their lives would be easier if they applied the principles you have learned. We would ask that you please be patient and understand that they are exactly where they are supposed to be in their spiritual path and development right now. They are where you were earlier in your quest for spiritual knowledge and really require nothing from you. Attempting to help others who are not yet ready to learn does not serve either party. You may even prolong their resistance to opening up to their spirit self, so always keep that in the forefront of your mind and accept each person as they show up to you. Hold them in your love; by doing so, you can show them what love can provide them.

Many are just now awakening to the possibility that there is something they do not know about themselves. They may begin to reach out to those around them to ask questions.

When this type of opportunity presents itself to you, you will know that you can speak to them. Make sure that you step aside and allow the Holy Spirit to speak through you, as He will know exactly what to say to them in answer to any questions they may have. The Holy Spirit can reach them at the exact place where they are and speak to them in a way that allows them to hear the message.

It is important to remember that each person has a free will and can choose otherwise in their path in this lifetime. There is nothing wrong with making these choices. Please do not judge anyone nor make them wrong. They will have many new opportunities to expand their spiritual knowledge both in this and future lifetimes. Rejoice in the knowledge that all is exactly as it should be and that they will attain their full spiritual potential in exactly the right timing for them. You are all on this planet to grow spiritually, and each person will grow in exactly the right moment for them.

Those who are not yet awakened can learn from witnessing those who are living through their true spirit selves. These are the ones who learn by observing others. They will observe the peace, love, and joy that radiates from those who are living from love. They may begin to wonder how they may incorporate the peace, love, and joy they see emanating from you into their lives. Be the image they strive to be, and hold that image for them until they are ready to step into that space. They will see it and naturally want to know what you are doing to feel that way about life.

Lovingly holding an image of enlightenment for someone is the best means of helping those who are closest to you in your life and are not yet awakened. Free yourself as well as them from any expectations you may have of them. Love and admire them for who they are today and know that their path is unfolding in front of them and is exactly as it should be right now. When you can love all those who show up to you unconditionally, you have learned the core concept of living in Oneness. When you accept others where they are right now, you allow them to move forward at their own pace. Bask in the love that is you and enjoy each moment, as that is who you really are.

Oneness operates out of the belief that We are all one and made from God's energy. This is the universal truth of our existence.

Chapter 8
Fourth-Dimensional Living

Understanding Physical Dimensions

In the universe there are twelve dimensional planes of physical incarnation, or what We refer to as manifestation. There are thousands of planets in the universe that support life and physical manifestation. There are many planets that are vibrating at the third and higher dimensional levels. Earth is moving from vibrating at the third dimension to vibrating at the fifth dimension. The transition from the third to the fifth dimension will take many years to complete, as the energy level increases are incremental in order for Earth to more comfortably endure the process. To understand the ascension process to higher dimensions, you need to understand the relationship of the vibrational dimension of the planet to the spiritual ascension of its inhabitants.

Each planet vibrates at a predetermined dimensional range of energy frequencies, but its inhabitants typically range in spiritual ascension levels from one to two dimensions above or below the planet's frequencial dimension. For example, your planet is currently vibrating at the third dimensional level, but your inhabitants range in spiritual ascension levels from the third through fifth dimensions. The range in frequencies allows for your spiritual growth from dimension to dimension within the boundaries of your frequencial planet. It allows for your growth even when you are having a difficult time raising your own energy

On December 12, 2012, your planet began to further increase its energy from a third- to a fifth-dimension planet in vibrational frequency. The process of raising Earth's energy fully to the fifth-dimensional level will take approximately twenty-five years and will be complete in 2038. Although many of your advanced teachers, healers, and messengers have already begun their ascension, the majority of your inhabitants will begin their ascension to higher spiritual dimensions beginning in 2013. Those who are at the third dimensions will begin to transition toward the fourth dimensions, and those who are at the fourth and fifth spiritual dimensions will continue their transition toward the fifth and sixth dimensions respectively.

Approximately 85 percent of your planet is currently vibrating in the third-dimensional realm and will now begin their transition to the fourth dimension. Although your planet will be vibrating fully at a fifth-dimensional level by 2038, it will take hundreds of years before the majority of people on your planet are at a fifth-dimensional spiritual level or higher. It is our hope that within three hundred years, at least 85 percent of your inhabitants will be at the fifth through seventh spiritual dimensions. The timing can be shorter or longer, depending upon how receptive and eager your societies are to adopt the Universal Divine Laws. To remain in the fifth dimension you will need to continue to live by them. Again, it is, as always, a matter of free will and the choices that each person makes that moves that person along on his or her path.

Becoming Who You Really Are

There are many ways of being in Oneness. Oneness operates out of the belief that We are all one and part of God's energy, and that is a fact. To fully live in Oneness, each person must shed the cloak of individuality and stay focused within the truth that We are all interconnected. Remember that We are individuations of God's energy, united in Oneness and indivisible in all your physical and non-physical glory. When I say *We,* I am referring to all beings in the physical dimensions as well as all energy within the spiritual realms. I am describing all of God's energy. All energy is interlaced and interrelated. Your interconnected energy extends on into infinity. It intermingles with all other energy and never fades. Because you are interconnected, your emotional states and everything that you think, say, and do affects all who are around you. If you are vibrating from the emotional frequencies of love, peace, and Oneness, then you positively affect all that is around you. If you are vibrating at the lower emotional levels of sadness, regret, shame, guilt, unforgiveness, and blame, then you are affecting those around you in negative ways. Now that you know this Universal Divine Law, what emotions will you choose to be part of your life? Will you choose to be a positive influence on your family, coworkers, and friends, or will you choose to affect them negatively?

You are singly responsible for all the thoughts and emotions that you project out into the world. When you project positive emotions out into the world, you will experience positive events and emotions coming back to you. When you project negative emotions out into the world, you will experience negative events and emotions coming back to you. That is the nature of karma and living in your physical world. There is nothing you can do to change these Universal Divine Laws, but you always have the option to change your thoughts about your world. Ask yourself, "Do I want the problem or do I want the answer?" Ask to know the answer and it will be provided to you.

As you progress in the fourth dimension, you will begin to notice that you spend less and less time in your negative emotions. When you lose the feelings and emotions of Oneness, you will want to reconnect as soon as possible. As always, you have free will and choices in how you choose to be in your daily life. Remember, when you change your perspective, you change your life. Take a moment to step back to recognize the choices you have made so far today. How did you do on your path of Oneness? If you found you made mistakes, please don't be hard on yourself. Reflect with self-love and honor the process. Now consider what you will choose for tomorrow. There, see? It is not so difficult to choose Oneness. Moreover, by making new loving choices, you clear the karma created by lesser choices. Isn't love wonderful?

Understanding the Fourth Dimension

Most on your planet believe they have many ways of being in your world, but there is really only one way of being. Either you are living your life from the emotion of love or you are living it from fear. When you choose to live from love, your life will reflect positive emotions through your thoughts, words, and actions. The emotions that come from being in the frequency of love are peace, joy, happiness, passion, excitement, honor, and compassion, and they flow from you. These emotions create the greatest possibility of positively influencing all those around you. This now becomes your natural state of *being*, and anything less will no longer be accepted within your holy mind. What a gift you can become just by *being* in these positive emotions around others. While in the energy of love, you have the potential to help your fellow brothers and sisters every time you are around them. You are love and have the ability to expand your feelings of love to those around you, which helps them move their energy levels up to their frequency of love.

Practice this exercise as a prayer each night before you go to sleep, and you will positively and profoundly affect your world. You may wish to teach it to your children so that they can learn how they can positively affect their world. As you get ready for the prayer, recall a special memory from your past when you felt complete and unconditional love for another person, and hold that feeling in your heart space. Now ask God to help you expand and send out that love to your family and friends. Then continue to increase and expand that love to cover your entire city, then state, then country, then planet Earth, and then the entire universe. Now send out peace to surround Earth and the universe. Finally, send out harmony to surround Earth and then the universe. Make no exceptions in this prayer, and ensure that you have included yourself in this love, peace, and harmony. What a beacon of love you are at that moment! When you pray and live your life this way, you cannot help but have good flow into your life."

Your Shift into the Fourth Dimension

The fourth dimension is the dimension where the enlightened begin to create within Oneness and are shifting from using their egoic thought systems into living from their spirit selves. Your Earth is vibrating at a higher dimensional vibration, which provides an easier opportunity for you to grow spiritually and even exceed these new frequencies. The fourth dimension can best be described as a transitional dimension. It is the place where you can move away from your egoic world by learning, understanding, and practicing the new ways of *being* that are required for living in a fifth-dimensional world. Simply put, the fourth dimension prepares you to live in the fifth-dimensional realm. What a grand opportunity to become the highest expression of God's Love for all those who enter your life. Life is about to become what you have thought impossible for so many of your lifetimes. Cherish the process of learning and growing. Make it fun. Enjoy every part of it as you grow to be the person you are intended to *be*.

As you awaken to the truth of who you are as a child of God, your perceptions will shift as well, and you will begin to remember your connectedness. In the fourth dimension, it will become easier to remain in the higher emotional frequencies as you feel more connected to everyone around you. You begin to see the world through new eyes and interpret what you see from the new perspectives of your connectedness. Your choices begin to reflect this new perspective as you consider new ways of being in your daily lives. You choose to assist others where there was never a thought to this before. You feel love much more intensely, and you cannot contain the joy of feeling this way. You smile more often at the simple things in life and thoroughly appreciate that they are there for you to enjoy.

As you fully awaken to who you are as a child of God, you will step into your purpose for being here at this time. You may also begin to remember and see past-life events that have special meaning to you now. You will remember that you are not of Earth and that you came here a long time ago from another place to help the people of Earth move back up to a fifth-dimensional world. You will reflect on your many lifetimes, their purposes, and how you pursued them. You will also see those where you didn't remember and lived out your life in forgetfulness. Only the learning and love will remain with you from these lifetimes as you appreciate what they have to offer you.

In the higher Earth energy, it will be easier to remember your purpose and hear your spirit guides provide you with guidance each day. Seize the opportunities that are available to you at this very special period of ascension. You can accomplish in this lifetime what would normally have taken many lifetimes to achieve. Most important, do it with love, joy, and laughter. Advancement without joy doesn't truly serve you. You are meant to enjoy every aspect of your life, so seize the moment with the joy, loving intention, and innocence of a child at play.

Your Purpose in the Fourth Dimension

You've waited a long time to be a part of what is occurring now. Many of you left your home planets more than 100,000 years ago to be a part of helping the Earth move to a fifth-dimensional planet. Your work here is almost complete while Earth shifts from a third- to a fifth-dimensional planet. The process of change and evolution will take many years. Some of you may wish to complete your work on Earth in this lifetime and then return to your home planet in your future lifetimes. Others may choose to stay on Earth and continue your work here in future lifetimes. It is all a matter of choice, and We are very grateful for and honor you for everything you have accomplished.

There are many ways that you may choose to live in the fourth dimension. To say that change is required is an understatement. Moving from your third-dimensional egoic thought system to *being* in the fourth dimension will require you to break down old patterns of thought and how you react to others. Your ego has been in charge of your thoughts, words, and actions for so long now that you may be on automatic pilot within this process. To shift from your egoic thought system to one guided by your spirit self, you will need to be mindful of your thoughts and how you process them in every moment of each day. That is a tall order for anyone to accomplish. That was the purpose of *A Course in Miracles*. I will now ask that you consider working with it if you have not already done so. This book allows you to practice stepping away from your egoic thoughts and seeing your world as it truly is. It will gently guide you toward awakening your fourth-dimensional self and prepare you to venture into the fifth realm of *being*. If you have previously read *A Course in Miracles* and completed the exercises contained in the workbook, I would ask that you consider rereading it once again in the hopes that you may find more meaning in it now.

Awakening Your Gifts

The fourth dimension allows humans to live at the level of being connected to the Universal Divine Knowledge and Universal Consciousness. Many on your planet have been at this level previously and were able to connect to other realms during most of your Earth's history. These are the masters, messengers, healers, and enlightened individuals who have reached connectedness to the Universal Divine Consciousness and Universal Divine Knowledge. They were sent to remind each generation to come back to understand their connectedness to God and all that is in the universe.

The fourth dimension allows your spirit self to merge with your body and to become one. This is the next level in your evolutionary migration and requires mind, body, and spiritual changes to occur for all those on your planet. This is a very important step in your advancement, as it allows for constant connection to the Universal Divine Consciousness and all that is available to you within it. With the merger of your spiritual self with your body, you will eventually ascend to higher dimensions and be able to transcend your Earthly realm and connect to other consciousness and those that have passed.

You will eventually acquire many other abilities, but attaining them requires your further advancement in spirituality. It is very important that you understand that with these new abilities comes great responsibility. You will acquire these new abilities only as you move up in your spirituality to the degrees necessary for you to understand the purpose and true nature of each ability, and retained the wisdom and responsibility to use them wisely. It is through honoring these gifts that you are able to receive the blessings contained within them.

Clearing Karma and Energy Distortion

The multidimensional world that is birthing right now on your planet will bring with it much responsibility. The new powers that you will have will require you to truly live in Oneness so that these gifts will not be abused. Living authentically in Oneness will require rethinking how you live each day. The next book that I write with this author will contain specific ideas and examples of how you may choose to live on this planet moving forward.

It will not be an easy time during this transition, as there will be many who resist these changes. The process of shedding the third-dimensional egoic thought system requires each person to release any unresolved karma and energetic distortion that has built up from this lifetime and past incarnations. Those who are attached to their egoic ways will not understand what is occurring, and this will create much fear within them. As an outcome of this fear, there may be periods of unrest until there is a tipping point of positive energy flowing from all those enlightened on your planet.

Energetic distortion carries fears and erroneous beliefs forward from previous lifetimes within your energy field. These distortions may still be playing out for you in this lifetime. You may have been a victim of mental, physical, or sexual abuse in previous lives, and if not recognized and cleared, these events may continue to play out in this and future lifetimes. The way to clear these distortions is to ask the Holy Spirit to show you these events. Then ask your soul self what you are to learn from these them. Once you understand what you need to learn, you can choose to live your life moving forward from the new perspective you have gained. Having worked through these events, you can choose to release the distortions and free up that energy for living your life more fully in Oneness.

Is there an event that keeps occurring in your life that you can't seem to understand, change, or put behind you? Look back on your life. What patterns keep occurring over and over again in your relationships? Perhaps it is a power struggle you keep having with significant others in your life. Or do you have a difficult time accepting the authority of others? Do you sometimes feel you are not good enough? Do you feel you don't fit in? Are you afraid all the time? These repeating scenarios and emotions are indicators that a major event has affected this or previous lives. They may also be associated with false beliefs you have about yourself. When these repeating events and emotions arise for you, please extend love to these events and emotions. Surround the fear or negative belief with your love and ask, "What it is that I need to learn from this?" If this doesn't provide you with relief, then you may ask the Holy Spirit to help you remove these patterns of distortion from your life. Moreover, in the asking, release will be given to you.

During these periods of remembering, learning, and clearing, many different emotions will come up. These emotions are there for a reason. They are there to help you awaken to your true self and all the possibilities that are available to you. Please don't look at these events as something bad. Instead, see them as an opportunity to grow spiritually, and then release them so that you can have a future that is different from your past. In your past, you had limited awareness, and as you are now awakening, you can begin to see other options. Now that you know this, you can choose the most loving choice for all parties involved.

You are learning to understand that all your emotions spring from your thoughts, words, and actions and manifest for you. Currently, and in your past, you have had negative thoughts and have said and done things that were unloving. Remember my previous teachings, which explained that whatever you do to another or yourself comes back to you through karmic law.

When these karmic experiences and past-life distortions come back to you, they are intended to raise your awareness of how you showed up in your past and how others felt during these events. These events are there for you to learn how to better use love to transcend your past. Ask yourself, "What could I have done to show up more lovingly in these events?" And in transcending your past with love, you will leave your fears behind you.

During this process of learning, some of you will be confused and not understand why this person or that event happened to you. Remember that there are no coincidences. Rest assured that these people or events are there for a reason, and your soul self knows this to be true. There is a purpose for you in these events, and you will continue to re-experience these karmic instances until you remember that you are love and understand what you were meant to learn from these experiences. If you are unaware and not conscious of the effects of karmic laws, then the experience will continue to show up for you until you are ready to remember, understand, learn from, and release these energies.

This process of recognizing what is occurring, learning from it, and then releasing it allows you to embrace your new life in the fourth dimension. During these periods of learning, you may be inundated with memories of your past. These memories have come up to you to bring you opportunities to release these experiences. It is at these times that you can choose to move forward or stay stuck in your drama. These memories are intended to serve as tools to examine how you have lived in the past, and then realize what worked and what didn't. You can then lovingly choose the highest and best good for all involved moving forward. This is the new way to *be* in Oneness.

You have also experienced many times where you were very loving, and by karmic law that comes back to you as well. What you do lovingly for another comes back to you many-fold from the universe. It won't necessarily come back to you from the person that you bestowed your love upon, but it will come back to you nonetheless. As your awareness of your Oneness becomes more pronounced in your daily life, you will experience more and more loving events. Your loving thoughts, words, and actions also serve to raise you up in your spiritual ascension and move you closer to God.

If you are troubled or feel stuck, seek assistance from Me or the Holy Spirit. It is our purpose to help you grow spiritually and experience great joy in your lives. Once you have reached the state of continued Oneness, you can now rise above the effects of karma. As a being of love, you will have transcended the need for balancing karma.

This process of spiritual growth will continue to evolve over and over again until you reach the highest point of growth and merge back into that energy which is pure God. You may then decide to remain a part of God for a while. Then you can decide to individuate once more and descend to re-experience the ascension process all over again. In the Divine Universe there are many choices of who, what, when, where, and how that can occur for you, each with its unique challenges and benefits. This is your truth and what is real in the universe. It is a wonderful progression of love and creation."

The fifth dimension is not only a new frequency realm; it is a state of being. Living in the fifth dimension allows each of you to engage with everyone else at a level where all are actively co-creating and cooperating within all aspects of your daily lives.

Chapter 9
Fifth-dimensional Living

The Fifth Dimension

The fifth dimension is not only a new frequency realm; it is a state of being. Living in the fifth dimension allows each of you to engage with everyone else at a level where all are actively co-creating and cooperating within all aspects of your daily lives. It requires a major shift in your consciousness, so that instead of "thinking with your ego," you engage only your spirit self for all input on your next actions. You will automatically access the Divine Consciousness for information, ideas, and input, and to answer any questions. You will also process any incoming information from your spirit self. Then you can act upon this information as you seek to attain your intended goal. This allows you to see all as it truly is, without the need to categorize, define, or judge what is occurring.

It is this shift to automatically accessing and processing information from the Divine Consciousness that places you within the fifth-dimensional state of being. This is your goal. We are here to assist you with your process of transition from the third into the fourth and finally *being* within the fifth dimension. Know that there will be times where you will be challenged to remain connected in Oneness, and at times, you may even want to allow your ego to take over. It is at this point that you will need Us the most. We ask you to remember that We are only a thought away and available to assist you through what you are experiencing. Ask and it will be given to you.

For those who would like to collapse time in your spiritual development, it can be done in this lifetime. It requires you to be constantly mindful of what thought processing engine

you are using in each moment of every day. You will want
to ask yourself, "Am I experiencing this moment from my
ego or from my spirit self?" At first, you will need constant
reminders to stay connected through your spirit self in all that
you think, say, and do. However, with practice, it will become
second nature to you, and you will be living in Oneness.

Once you have fully internalized Oneness and are working
exclusively from your spiritual Christed self, you will
have ascended to the fifth dimension. If you complete your
intended purpose, you can ask the Holy Spirit what else you
can do for your spiritual growth. And in the asking, you will
be shown what options are available for you to choose. What
a glorious accomplishment for you to achieve. The joy and
happiness you will experience as an outcome of your hard
work will not be able to be contained and will spill out to
affect others around you. You will have become a beacon of
light for others to follow, for they will want to experience the
joy they see flowing from you.

Fifth-dimensional Being

Fifth-dimensional Oneness is the state of being where you are
connected to the Divine Consciousness and are taking your
instructions from the Divine. The ego is not engaged in this
process. It does not filter, process, or insert information. You
are merely listening from your spirit self to what you need to
know and/or do for that moment or that day. As you seek to
know how to be in each moment, the highest benefit and best
outcome for you can flow from the Divine to you. Your ego
could not possibly know what is around each corner or how
an event will play out, but the Divine Consciousness does
and can guide you onto the path that is in alignment with
your purpose for being here. This path will also bring the
greatest joy into your life. It is at this point in time that you
will realize your Oneness with God and everything else in the
universe.

Love is Oneness. Unconditional love is the primary emotion
of *being* in Oneness. If you are feeling any emotion other
than love and the positive feelings that flow from love, you

are not in Oneness. As you grow in spirituality, you will begin to associate true joy, ecstasy, happiness, and other high-frequency emotions with Oneness, and you will be correct. These emotions are the outcome of giving love unconditionally while being of service to others. When you are of service to others, and this service is motivated only by unconditional love, you are in Oneness. However, if you are motivated by the desire for some sort of recognition or praise or have a private agenda for your actions, you are operating out of your ego. You are giving to get, and that is the ego at work. Although your actions will be notable and worthy, you will not have the benefits of the deep feelings of joy and happiness. Why would you put yourself in such a place? Learn to give unconditionally for the pure joy of giving, and then enjoy the love and joy that comes back for you to experience once again.

Connecting with Others

There are infinite possibilities that come from living in Oneness, and this book cannot address all of them. There are so many things you could do differently that would benefit all on your planet. Regardless of the circumstances that present themselves to you, consider accepting those with love in your heart. Then visualize the outcome to become a win/ win for everyone involved, and that is what will occur. When realized in this fashion, your lives could play out with such a joyous outcome that once you have begun to experience living it, you will never want to go back to how life used to be for you. While living in Oneness, you will feel the joy of having a depth of connectedness with others, which you have not known in many millennia. You will have the ability to completely understand the point of view of another and then be able to accommodate both your wishes and theirs for a solution where all benefit. This knowing and trusting one another on a soul level will have amazing healing power for all of humankind.

Your world will soon be different, and how you view others will change considerably. Many of you will change your occupations, and your lives will change accordingly. People have already begun to shift to new occupations and careers based upon their purpose for being here, and this trend will continue over the next twenty to thirty years. Do not be tempted to compare yourself with others or how your life was previously. This too would be coming from your egoic thought system and may create negative thought patterns for you. What your ego thought you should do, versus what you really would like to do coming from your heart, in many cases will be divergent. There are also many who will continue working right where they are, as they have already chosen their life purpose path. Allow the Holy Spirit to guide you with any possible shift in occupation so that you can attain the highest and best outcome for all those connected to your life.

As you gain in experience and understanding on how to spiritually connect to individuals in your life on a soul level, you will begin to transfer that knowledge to other groups of people. This occurs for most through observation. As your circle of influence increases, it will grow to include people of different religions, cultures, beliefs, and nationalities. Misconceptions about others will dissolve, and you will see them for who they really are. Instead of seeing their differences, you will focus on what you have in common, and from this perspective, you will be able to solve many of the problems facing your planet. The problems that will be resolved include ensuring that every man, woman, and child on your planet has a place to live, proper clothing to wear, healthful food to eat, fresh water to drink, full access to needed natural resources, and an education. Let the Holy Spirit guide you as to which modalities are appropriate for each person, as each will have a unique purpose. Most important, they will feel the love and connectedness that is their inheritance from all their fellow brothers and sisters on your new Christed Earth.

Doing Business in the Fifth Dimension

The shift to the fifth dimension will affect how businesses operate in the world, and their products will mirror their love. With many choosing to live their lives from their spirit self, your world will reflect the good intentions of all those who do business with you. They will want to ensure that you are happy with their products and services. They will understand that natural resources are precious and meant to be protected. From this knowing, they will ensure that all products are built to the highest quality standards, so they last much longer and are made from resources that are plentiful and recyclable.

In your fifth-dimensional world the more joyful you are in your work environment, the more you positively affect those around you. The reverse is also true. The unhappier you are in your work, the more negatively you will affect others. If you are unhappy doing the work that you are doing, it will be both yours and your manager's responsibility to find a position that better serves you and your purpose. In realizing that joy in the workplace creates a positive effect on the company and all those around you, your managers will want to shift unhappy workers to new positions they more thoroughly enjoy and appreciate while still serving their purpose. If there are egoic issues, then perhaps counseling or energy work would be made available to help them regain their balanced essence.

In the fifth dimension, your planet will shift completely away from individuals climbing the corporate ladder to become those *being* what gives them purpose. Your happiness will come from lovingly performing your purpose versus what would pay you the highest income. You will no longer focus on what you can buy, but instead focus on the quality of your relationships and how you can be of service to others. You will have come to realize that your joy comes from the connectedness of your many loving relationships, and all else will cease to be of importance to you.

Opening Doors to the Universe

Once your planet has accomplished sustained global connectedness on a soul level, you will be ready to learn more about your connectedness with the remainder of the universe in which you live. Doorways to other planets and universes will become known to you in the future, and you will benefit from learning what other higher-dimensional planets have to teach you. These doorways will become available only once it has been determined that it is safe to do so for the other planets in your galaxy and the universe. With greater abilities come greater responsibility for ensuring the highest and best outcome of all actions and all those involved.

There is much you can learn from other planets, and in the next few chapters I will describe for you some of the ways in which they live. You would benefit greatly from them. In the not-too-distant future, you will invite them to come here to help you move more fully into the fifth dimension. You will also travel to other planets to observe and live amongst them, which will provide powerful insights to those willing to take this step forward. Only those who have advanced to the higher levels of spiritual growth, awareness, and responsibility will be allowed to visit other planets. The rewards of being able to take this step into other worlds are immense and will bring great joy and a higher sense of community. They are, indeed, your brothers and sisters in every way. They are as excited as you are for your worlds to merge into community with each other. This will truly be a glorious time for everyone in your galaxy."

What you do for another, you do for yourselves. What you do for nature, you do for yourselves. What you do for all living beings, you do for yourselves. In forgiving another, you are forgiven. In giving unconditional love, you receive unconditional love. In healing another, you are healed. In bringing joy to another, you receive joy.

Chapter 10
Understanding Oneness

Earth History and Oneness

As some of you may know, every 25,920 years Earth
completes its circumnavigation in the Milky Way galaxy, and
that is when its connectivity to God is at its highest point. The
higher energy flowing into Earth helps all beings be more
closely connected to the Universal Divine Consciousness.
This period of highest connectivity lasts approximately
two thousand years, and then the energy begins to slowly
decrease until it is at its lowest point. In the midcycle of the
25,920-year circumnavigation, (12,960 years) Earth is at
its farthest point from the Divine energy. This period also
lasts approximately two thousand years, and then the energy
begins to increase until the cycle is completed once again. It is
when you are at the farthest point that many beings lose their
connection to God. Many forget who they are as children
of God and perceive everything through their egos. These
periods of darkness have caused advanced societies in your
past to become prey to those who were living from power,
greed, jealousy, blame, and hate.

The concept of Oneness is not new to your Earth. Many
societies have lived that way in your history when the
energy was at its highest. Atlantes, LeMuria, and Rama-Mu
were the most advanced societies thus far on your planet.
These advanced star-seeded societies lived this way for
approximately 300,000 years. They were far more advanced
than your societies today, in spirituality, social order, and
advanced technologies. These societies were brought down
by jealous and power-hungry groups who looked to do much
harm on this and other planets. When these great societies
became threatened, many enlightened ones moved from
these cities and formed other similar societies around the

world. The natural disasters, social unrest, and wars that destroyed these great societies all originated from negative egoic thoughts of power, greed, jealousy, blame, and hate. Their negative egoic thoughts produce discontent and lead to thoughts, words, and actions that are more negative. When they were left unchecked, their social patterns spiraled down into more negative emotions, words, and actions. Then they became more and more disintegrated. Eventually, these societies forgot who they were as children of God and became completely detached from God. If you are proactive, then this disconnection will not occur again when Earth is at the farthest point from the Divine energy, at its next midpoint of circumnavigation.

The enlightened ones who moved from these cities founded smaller communities that remembered who they were. You know these people today as the indigenous peoples who were living off the land throughout your continents during your history. Through all these years, they have continued to carry the light of truth and remembered that they are connected and had a purpose for being on Earth. Their light has now spread to the ends of Earth, and because of their persistence, many are now awakening to the truth of their existence. Their light is growing brighter as the energy of your planet is increasing, and many more are awakening on a daily basis. This is truly a great time for your planet. Rejoice, as these light keepers have succeeded in bringing your planet back into connection with the Divine, and your planet is now ready to ascend back up to the fourth, then fifth dimension.

Understanding Oneness

Understanding Oneness begins with absolutely knowing that We are all One with God, and that you are as God created you.

We are all interconnected, and as such:
What you do for another, you do for yourselves.
What you do for nature, you do for yourselves.
What you do for all living beings, you do for yourselves.
In forgiving another, you are forgiven.

> In giving unconditional love, you receive unconditional love.
> In healing another, you are healed.
> In bringing joy to another, you receive joy.

Those who are awakening at this time are beginning to understand the universal laws that are operating at all times in the universe. You are beginning to grasp that your thoughts can manifest. You are just beginning to remember all that you are capable of doing when living from your spirit self. If you are just now awakening, take the time to learn what manifestation is and how to use it in positive ways. Manifesting is much of who you are. It will greatly enhance your lives. Become a student once again. Purposely incorporate the universal laws into your lives. Ask your spirit guides to teach you how to be in Oneness, and they will joyfully comply with your requests.

Being in Oneness

The main way of accepting Oneness is through knowing you are in Oneness. This is done through your feelings. It is a strong feeling of love and an absolute knowing that you are ONE with all there is. It is through this knowing that you will come to understand your connectedness with the Universal Consciousness of God. Communicating within the Divine Consciousness can also be a part of your daily living. There are many ways to receive the information coming from the Universal Divine Consciousness.

Many on your planets receive their Divine communication through meditation. They also receive messages as a feeling or knowing or intuition. For some it may show up as strong emotions that urge them to do certain things. Many others are clairaudient and can hear the messages either audibly or through a voice inside their head. Others are clairvoyant and can see images either through their third eye or as three-dimensional opaque displays. Others are telepathic and receive thoughts from Divine source. Please understand that these abilities are not special. Everyone has these innate Divine gifts. When you are ready to embrace your spirituality, these gifts will be awakened within you.

Your connectedness is a high vibrational energy that puts you
in the realm of God. Being in the realm of God allows you
to embrace and understand all there is. Once you are living
your true connectedness, the egoic beliefs that you previously
had will no longer make sense to you. You will come to
understand who you are within Oneness, and then you will
no longer wish to consider yourself as an independent being.
You will want to assist others in this knowing so that they
may share Oneness and the joy of connectedness. Please
be understanding of where others are on their journey and
remember that they will need to show up as a student to you
first, before they are ready to learn. And when you show up as
their teacher, that is when your true learning begins. (As you
teach, you learn.)

Ascending to Oneness

The goal of the current shifts in the energy on your planet
is to assist all in ascending. This requires a shift in your
spiritual awareness so that you may begin to actually live in
Oneness. For some of you beginning the ascension process
this will be fairly painless, and you can progress rather
quickly once you understand the universal Divine laws and
begin the process. The key to entering the ascension process
is to forgo the egoic thought system in exchange for listening
to your spirit self. Although that may sound fairly easy, most
will have a very difficult time with this transition.

Many of you will begin the process with great joy and
fortitude, but will quickly realize that with real life
experiences coming at you daily, it is more difficult than it
first appeared. Do not despair; it is a process of trial and error
and ultimately joy. Initially, through a natural ebb and flow,
you will vacillate back and forth between egoic thoughts and
your spiritual self for periods of time, until you have learned
the means of really *being* and REMAINING within the spirit
self. It will get easier as the energy of your planet increases.
A few important things to consider as you go through these
phases: Be kind and gentle with yourself and others as each
of you traverse up and down through these phases of learning
and *being*. It is a process of change and, as such, requires

repeated practice before it becomes second nature to you.
Use meditation to gently lift you out of frustration or other
negative emotions that keep you from joy. Use calming music
to help you and others remain in the highest vibrational
energies. You are meant to enjoy the process and all that it
brings to you, so keep that in mind as you begin your journey.
Laughter is always good medicine for your soul, so do your
learning playfully.

Know and understand that you are going to get sucked back
into egoic thoughts repeatedly as you are faced with difficult
and familiar situations. Know this, recognize it, and quickly
forgive yourself and others in this challenging stage of
transition. Learn to laugh and have fun with the process, and
it won't be as difficult for you, your families, or friends. As
you progress in your learning, you will find that the egoic
voice inserts itself less and less, and when it does, it will not
last as long or be as severe. This is an experience that you
have chosen, and with time, you will complete it and move
on to other joyous experiences. It is with great delight that
We watch you ascending, for We know the rewards you will
receive as an outcome of your work. We are here to assist
you and love it when you call upon Us for help. We are only a
thought away and will playfully engage you if you wish.

Your Purpose in Oneness

Before coming down to Earth, each of you intended to
have certain experiences in this lifetime. In your blueprint
for this incarnation, each major event was planned. Your
purpose is always the extension of love, but how it plays out
is highly individualized for each incarnation. These planned
experiences required others to show up in your life for
certain periods of time. These periods of interaction include
the opportunity for each of you to grow and learn during
your relationship. In addition to the other aspects of your
purpose, EACH of you is here at this very important time
in your Earth's history to assist with the ascension of your
planet. Within your free will you may choose to accept each
planned experience the first time it is presented to you or not.
If you choose not to complete the intended experience when

planned, then the same experience will be presented to you again and again with either the same being(s) or others until you are ready to choose to complete the experience.

In reflecting on your life, perhaps you can see how repeated experiences have kept showing up for you. Notice how each of these repeated events has played out and how you were finally able to complete the experience. In reflection, you may even find that some may not be complete yet. Remember that each person shows up in your life as part of your experience. There are no accidents in life. Recognize the gift that each person provides you in your learning. When there is discord, consider that there is another option for you to choose in these events. You may choose to step back and ask for Divine assistance in helping you complete each of these experiences. Ask the Holy Spirit to help you know the highest and best outcome for all involved so that you may choose this option. This asking will enable you to reflect and understand what it is that you wished to experience. You will then traverse through them more easily and move on to different experiences.

Your path toward Oneness intersects with many others in this lifetime and through many lifetimes. As a unit, you and all those connected to you have chosen to travel certain sections of your paths together. These intersecting points are meant as a mutual spiritual benefit for each of you. Please note that you may not see everyone who comes into your life as a benefit, as some who cross your path will not bring you joy. But rest assured that they are there to bring you an experience you wished to undertake in order to advance yourself spiritually. Although their role may not appear to be one of love, they agreed to show up as requested by you so that you could complete these experiences.

If part of your path included experiencing the death of a loved one, then someone you love has to die and you must keep living. If you wished to experience being a victim, then someone had to be the perpetrator for you to know how a victim feels. Whether you believe it or not, all that you experience is 100 percent created by you. This is true for the victim, their perpetrator, and those they leave behind. You complete these experiences when you can feel unconditional love for everyone involved and have released all unforgiveness in the relationships. This forgiveness includes yourself and others for current and past events. You cannot hold on to any unforgiveness and claim you know Oneness.

It is also important to note that some of your life events will have additional consequences outside of spiritual growth. Your societies have laws and processes for those who break the rules. If you were the perpetrator, then you will live both the karmic and legal consequences of your actions. Or you may be required to testify or judge others within the legal requirements of your societies. We would ask that you do so with love and forgiveness in your hearts. The need to judge and sequester those who would harm others will become less and less necessary as you move closer to the fifth dimension and more people embrace Oneness. No matter the event or the outcome, thank those involved for the experience they brought through to your spirit self, as they have fulfilled their role as part of your purpose for being here.

Once you and those you encounter have had the chosen experience, then you each may choose to travel forward on the same or different paths within your Oneness in this lifetime. Be kind to yourself and to all others who show up in your life. Know that each interaction will eventually be played out exactly as the experience was intended and was initially set up with the highest and best outcome in mind for your purpose.

Your death or the death of a loved one is one of the most traumatic events a person or their family and friends can experience in physical life. The means of the death is immaterial, as no death occurs without your soul's permission. For most of you, the death of a loved one occurs within several scenarios of manifestation. I will list them below:

• The spirit self has completed their journey on Earth, and they have chosen to lay their body down as a completion of their purpose and an acceptance of the next experience awaiting them.

- A person dies of a disease that has unknowingly been self-inflicted through egoic thoughts of guilt. Guilt is fed by thoughts of separation, anger, hate, sin, and punishment, and it is made manifest through disease.

- The event was planned before your incarnation, such as the death of a child. This could be an accident, injury, or sudden death. The child's death would have been the completion of their life purpose, and could have the intention of leading the parents to ask why. In their searching, they learn the truth of their purpose in this lifetime. And in their continued search for answers, they learn to connect to their child on the other side of the veil, where the child gives them important messages for their purpose and continued spiritual growth.

- A person takes his or her own life. This event would occur as planned or not, depending upon whether the individual was coming from their spirit self through love or from their ego out of fear, anger, or pain. If it was a planned event, then it would have occurred as a means of helping another know their purpose and/or gaining spiritual growth and the completion of their purpose in this lifetime. Spiritual growth of those left behind can also occur, even when the event was unplanned.

Oneness in Advanced Societies

Although Oneness may physically show up as different practices for each species, their practices all originate from similar beliefs. Advanced societies have beliefs that are centered within their knowledge that they are part of the Universal Consciousness of God. They know they are all part of God's energy, that they are connected to each other, and what they do for another they are actually doing for themselves. They know this from birth, and it is not something they must learn.

In advanced societies, there is also a natural detachment from outcomes that each being feels. Their detachment typically circumvents any issues around expectations. Since they live in the now, neither their past nor their future is taken into consideration when choosing the next experience they wish to have. Each is free to manifest what they wish to experience on a daily basis, but they do so in a very responsible and honorable manner. Most do not plan very far into the future, as they may wish to leave their options open to experience new things. They realize they are each evolving and may have different wants in the future, which they don't currently know about.

Advanced societies live their lives with the knowledge that they are all one. And, as such, they consider all their actions as they relate to others, animals, plants, and their planet. There is a personal commitment to their community and doing one's part in maintaining its sustainability. They understand that they are the cause of all that is around them. Most look at the whole picture first to understand the effect of their thoughts, words, and actions on others and then choose to manifest what will reflect most positively for all involved. They live to bring joy to themselves as well as others.

These are not perfect societies, as many of these beings are also on varying levels of spiritual development. They all make mistakes as physical beings are inclined to do as part of their nature. They differ from your societies in that as long as they are living from their spirit selves with loving intent, they realize that any mistakes are easily recognized, acknowledged, and corrected. If they do make a mistake, they quickly choose to manifest a different, more positive reality once they see the negative effect of their prior decision. They accept responsibility for their actions without the blame or projection onto others that is so prevalent on your planet.

Most have learned to manifest in a pure way what they wish to experience in their daily lives. Their souls have progressed in their experiences to a point where they no longer wish to experience a society that isn't living consciously. Your planet is moving in that direction but has more to learn spiritually in order to get there. You are on the threshold of beginning your ascension toward the fifth dimension and will learn these principles and more as you move forward in your enlightenment.

Relationships in Oneness

Oneness in relationships is a difficult subject for many on your planet to understand at this time. Because you are given free will in all areas of your lives, there is a forgetfulness of the following:

- Who you really are

- That you are all connected

- How to love unconditionally

- How to manifest it in your life

Unconditional love is the means by which you live in Oneness. Unconditional love is allowing yourself to love everyone who comes into your life with complete acceptance and without judgment or expectations. It is the purest form of love. It's a realization that all who cross your path are there for a purpose; you are assisting them in an experience, or they are assisting you in your experiences.

Most of you think of relationships from the perspective of what you can gain from them. If you give something to a person, you expect them to give you something in return. These can be gifts of your love, time, help, friendship, money, or objects. For many of you these gifts are not gifts at all, as you have the expectation that eventually the person to whom you gave the gift will return the favor and present you with a gift of equal or greater measure. This is called giving-to-get and is not a part of unconditional love. Be honest with yourself, step back and reflect on the gifts you have given or received over your lifetime, and remember what your thoughts were at the time. Did you compare them with the ones that you gave or that were given by someone else? Did you measure them up against how you feel about this person? Were you disappointed? Alternatively, perhaps you felt an obligation to do something for them in return.

There is much for you to learn about the relationships in your life and giving. A true gift must be given without regard for anything in return. You are giving each gift out of unconditional love and do so to experience the joy of the person receiving the gift. True gifts are given unconditionally, with no strings attached. They are given to experience joy with the person receiving them, and that completes the experience. You may consider reflecting upon your relationships with your brothers and sisters, as they typically mirror your relationship with God. What is your relationship to God? How does it show up for you? Do you express joy, gratitude, and appreciation for all that you have?

Relationships and Fear

Fear is one of the most damaging aspects of any type of relationship. Most of your current relationships are lived through the lens of fear. Once you start a relationship, you immediately begin to fear losing it. The fear rises from within you, and you begin to believe that you must do something special to keep the person in relationship with you or they will leave. Once you have done things for them, you step back and wait for them to reciprocate to prove that they love you as much as you do them. Within this mind-set, you expect that they will want to stay in relationship with you because of all the things you have done for them. This is such a sad dance to watch you put yourselves through, and it is all so unnecessary. It would serve you well to also ask yourself why you are in each of your relationships. What purpose do they serve for you? Consider that as you live each day.

Relationships in advanced societies are unique in that they see the other beings as a reflection of themselves, so that whatever the other needs or wants usually becomes the giver's goal as well. There are no requirements to give or to reciprocate. They are unified in their want to help others experience all that they have come to their planet to experience. If they are so inclined to experience helping the other, they are free to do so or not, without judgment or expectations from anyone else or which path they choose. Each person is respected for who they are at each moment. They know that they can also choose to show up differently at any time in or out of the relationship as well. If one does not wish to experience the same event as another, then they may choose separate paths for a period of time or indefinitely. One doesn't take another's decision to stay or leave personally. Out of their mutual love they respect each other's right of free will and wish them well on their journey to experience all they have come to accomplish.

When someone is challenged by an experience, others may ask what they can do to help. The challenged person knows that they are coming from love and can then choose to respond with a list of ways in which they require help or say they do not need help at this time. Then the person helping may choose to either respond only in the manner(s) requested or not at all, depending upon what they wish to experience at that time. They do not consider doing anything for another except what was specifically requested for assistance. They also do not give help without receiving permission to do so ahead of time, as there is a high potential their actions would interfere with that person's planned experience. It could create negative karma for them as well.

In most cases the challenged person's wishes or requests are respected or granted, except when they may infringe upon what the helper wished to experience. If that is the case, then the helper is free to express that they do not wish to have that type of experience at this time, and the other respects that response without expectation or judgment. It is through this loving mutual respect that each being can feel safe and nurtured while they are able to realize all they wish to learn and experience. Each person in the interaction feels safe to express what is going on in their life and knows the other will treat them with respect, honor, and compassion during their interactions.

In the case of someone wishing to experience something that is potentially harmful to others and contrary to the experience others wished to have, there are opportunities for intervention. That could show up as someone standing up against the perpetrator or notifying authorities of what is about to occur. The authorities then discuss the situation with that being to either persuade them otherwise or prevent their moving forward. If necessary, means are put into place to protect those in harm's way. If the act is somehow completed, the individual is subject to the full legal consequences of their actions, as deemed appropriate by that society.

Friendships in Oneness

Most friendships on your planet are created out of mutual interest or goals. This is true in advanced societies as well. In most cases, friends will come into and out of your lives as a part of either you and/or them wanting to begin or continue to experience your relationship together. As long as all the parties wish to remain in the mutual experience, it will continue. Then you are free to choose whether or not to continue in this relationship doing something else or remain casually connected or move on to separate endeavors. These mutual experiences can be trivial or significant or anywhere in between.

If the relationship is significant, then this person probably made an agreement with you before coming down to your planet to be in this relationship. If it is a minor relationship, then more likely it was the bringing together of those in physical proximity with similar interests in response to a thought or wish or prayer for friendship. Remember that you manifest what you think (cause) so these people are there with you as a result (effect) of those previous thought(s). It is done in concert with their cause and effect as well.

In advanced societies, all relationships are given a Divine purpose, and friendships evolve or end as each person matures in their spirituality. They value everyone who comes into their lives because they know that they are there in response to their life plan or thoughts. They called these relationships forth; thus each of these people is highly respected and revered. In your societies, most of you are unaware that your thoughts manifest anything at all, let alone that someone would show up to engage you in an aspect of your life because you wished that experience to occur.

It is also important to understand that many of your negative experiences are in direct response to negative thoughts you have previously had as well. Thinking *All men are untrustworthy* would manifest with one or more men coming in and out of your life who are untrustworthy. If you continue to believe the same thought, this experience will continue to show up for you repeatedly until you choose a different thought about men to replace your previous beliefs. This is true for how your life plays out in all areas of your experiences and events. Remember, you can either consciously choose what you want to manifest or a choice will be made for you by default, through your egoic thoughts. Either way you are the sole creator of your reality, so choose wisely.

Romantic Relationships in Oneness

Romantic relationships are a source of much grief and jealousy in your societies. There is much confusion between attraction, and conditional and unconditional love in relationships. Most of you look at your romantic relationships with others as if you possess or own that person and have a right to determine what they do or don't do. It is from this perspective that you attempt to control all that they do and who they have as friends. Please note that any control or manipulation that is played out in your relationships will come back to you via karmic law, so choose wisely. The need for control stems from the egoic fear of loss. It is this fear of loss that creates the need to control or give-to-get, and these egoic tendencies are the strongest within romantic relationships. When a relationship is based upon fear or a giving-to-get mentality instead of one of unconditional love and respect, then you will not experience the love and joy you so very much desire. It is only through unconditional love that you can come to know and understand joy, happiness, and peace.

You are here to experience all that is available, and you are free to choose when, where, and how these experiences will occur. It is very important to make sure that all your relationships are acted out with unconditional love. In each interaction, you have the option to *be* the embodiment of God, which is unconditional love. Understanding the truth about relationships and unconditional love makes having a romantic relationship less about the ego and more about being in the present moment to enjoy all that is occurring in the now.

To truly be in the moment, you must experience it through your emotions, which forces you to *be* love, *be* joy, or *be* happy in the moment. Your emotions are what define the moment, as you are in truth choosing what you wish to experience at that time. You can also choose to *be* angry or *be* sad or *be* other negative emotions as well. It is always a choice, and it will play out however you have set it up to occur. When both parties know and accept this, then enjoying their physical presence and emotional connectedness can be a source of great joy and happiness for both parties. As with all relationships, the romantic relationship is intended to be lived coming from a common purpose. It may be to raise children together or to work on a common learning or healing experience together or a combination of these interactions. Please remember that all relationships are intended to bring you great joy, and that can come only from loving each other unconditionally.

You come together into romantic relationships to learn from certain issues that you cannot learn about in any other form. Some of these relationships are designed to play out for a lifetime, and others will end when the lessons have been learned and the experience completed. When a relationship ends, it should end with mutual love, respect, and knowing that the Holy Spirit has guided you to do so. Remember that you are always in relationship, even if that relationship is only with yourself. When you are out of relationship with others, this may very well be the period of time where you were intended to have enormous spiritual growth.

Let the Holy Spirit guide you with knowing how to deal with the events that occur in your relationships. All you need do is ask for assistance and listen in the quiet of your meditations to your response. Knowing that your relationship was intended to continue before a breakup could have helped you and your partner heal your hearts and go on to have rewarding closeness that was not there previously. Understanding what you were meant to learn and/or heal in the relationship will also help you understand why these events played out for you. How your romantic relationships play out is a matter of purpose for each of you. These relationships are typically planned out before your incarnation. You also planned events you wished to work through in order to understand how to better *be* the embodiment of God in these relationships. Ending these relationships early or forgoing the intended aspects of healing in the relationship will cause events or aspects of the relationship to repeat, until either one or both partners complete the intended experience. These repeated experiences can be quite frustrating when you don't understand that there is something you wanted to learn or heal in the relationship. Look for and recognize it when it's presented to you.

On the other hand, staying in a relationship that was not intended to continue or has any hope of allowing either party to learn or heal doesn't serve your purpose either. When these relationships no longer serve you or the other person, they can, in reality, block you from further spiritual growth. Whenever negative emotions are constantly present in a relationship, the love and joy can no longer be felt. It is then that you must choose whether you can get back to living within unconditional love and joy, or mutually and respectfully bow out of the relationship. Remember, you would do well to check in with your spirit self to learn and understand what is occurring and what you should do moving forward.

Keep in mind that a discordant relationship may be what you have come here to resolve, and that it may be in your best interest to continue the relationship to overcome the conflict. Check in with the Holy Spirit to understand what is occurring in your relationships. By reconnecting to the unconditional love you have for each other, the relationship can continue to play out to what was intended. In those relationships where unconditional love does not exist, you may be encouraged by the Holy Spirit to consider leaving. By leaving the relationship, each of you can provide the other with the potential to know unconditional love in a new relationship. You will know that leaving is the intended next step when both parties have worked with spirit and are in agreement that it is best for this to occur.

Romantic Relationships in Advanced Societies

In advanced societies lifelong romantic relationships are rare but do occur. They understand the intended purpose of their relationships, and they commit to each other for the duration of their mutual experience. As you do on Earth, they participate in commitment ceremonies. These events portray their desire to stay in a committed relationship for as long as they both mutually agree to do so. There is no "until death do us part" aspect to their commitment. Most beings come into and out of mutual relationships to complete experiences they wanted to occur at that time. There is no expectation for the other person to want to stay longer than what serves the intended experience for each of them. Both parties express their intent coming into the relationship, and there is mutual respect and acceptance when both of them mutually agree to end the relationship at some future time.

There is no drama or hard feelings when the relationship is ended. As with other relationships, they deeply respect and appreciate those who come into their lives to be a part of their experience. They value the time they spent together. They truly love the other unconditionally and wish them well when it is time for them to move on. There are no expectations that the relationship will endure over time. They live in the now and appreciate all that they have come together to experience. There is much love and acceptance of each other's need to move on, and they are sent on their way with love and blessings.

There is usually a period of time when one or both of the parties grieve the loss of the relationship, as it leaves a physical and emotion void in their lives. They consider grieving a natural part of the relationship process, just as you view grieving as natural upon the loss of a loved one or friendship on your planet. When one departs with love and acceptance, it leaves the door open for them to choose to be in relationship with each other again at some future date. The void they feel is looked upon as providing a space for a new experience to come into their life.

In advanced societies, almost all children are born into
committed relationships, and they remain intact until well
after the children are adults and living on their own. In
the rare cases where these relationships end and there are
young children involved, there is typically a desire to stay
in proximity to each other to maintain a loving and stable
parental relationship for the children. To maintain a close and
loving relationship with their children, ex-partners will often
choose to live in the same neighborhood or building together.
Their highest concern is for the children, and they each
support the best outcome for all involved. With that in mind,
many of these relationships usually continue as friendships
with many future shared experiences.

Platonic Male/Female Relationships in Oneness

Platonic male/female relationships can be a source of great
comfort and love. As with all other relationships, they are
formed out of a mutual consent for a common experience
together. The coming together of the male and female
essences allows each to gain the perspective of the other
sex in situations outside of a romantic relationship. In your
societies issues with these relationships tend to occur when
either or both of the parties are involved in a romantic
relationship. When the ego is allowed to run amok, jealousy
may occur. If that is the case, then the jealous party is living
out of an egoic fear of losing their romantic partner. If
they feel they own the other being, there are the additional
issues with possessiveness, manipulations, agreements, and
possessions.

In advanced societies there are no distinctions between male
and female friendships. All relationships are considered a
mutual coming together of individuals who wish to have an
experience together. Jealousy is a negative egoic emotion that
doesn't occur too often, but can come up in relationships. If
that is the case, then the parties come together to work out
their roles and how each will show up within the relationship
moving forward. Unconditional love, mutual respect,
compassion, and honor are the guiding emotions within

these relationships. When these emotions are present in the relationships, there is rarely a problem.

In many cases platonic relationships may occur after a romantic relationship has ended, usually when there is a need to come together for a mutual friendship or other benefit. These relationships may continue at the level of parenting, work, or mutual interest. Each is free to choose the experience they wish to have within these relationships, and either can choose to change the experience at any point. It is all lived out in the now. They don't tend to plan out their lives to the extreme like many do on your planet.

Sexual Relationships in Oneness

On Earth, sexual relationships are among the most misunderstood relationships. They typically involve much manipulation from one or both parties. Your religions have many rules and regulations around whom, how, and what can be done in a sexual relationship. Many on your planet cannot even say the word *sex* without feeling some level of discomfort, shame, or guilt. Sadly, there are many who have been taught to repress their sexual desires. From religions to schools and parents, all are living through the expectations and teachings of others, who learned from their parents and religions, and this problem has become epidemic. It is through this negative sexual repression that many turn to heinous crimes to release the tensions, shame, and guilt that sexual desires cause.

Another anomaly that shows up on your planet is that females and males are treated very differently in terms of sexual beliefs. Men are considered better men if they have had many sexual experiences, but women are treated poorly. In some locations, women are mutilated so that they cannot enjoy the sexual experience. You are also told to repress your sexual feelings from your early childhood, and yet your media bombards you with it on a daily basis. If one acts upon their sexual desires, they are judged and ridiculed for not having the fortitude to resist the "sin" of sexual expression. What God intended as a means to express unconditional love has become something that one does as a disassociated and unfeeling act. Please step back to see how far from unconditional love, honor, compassion, and excitement your sexual relationships have become.

You can have a loving sexual relationship without being in a committed relationship with the other person, although most in advanced societies choose to have sex within committed relationships. Their sexual desires are an outcome of their love for another, so wanting to more fully experience that relationship in commitment with each other is the next step in its progression. A loving sexual relationship in this sense means that you are acting with loving kindness, compassion, and excitement toward each other and intending the highest and best outcome for each person involved. The most important aspect of these mutually respected relationships is the heightened emotions that can be felt while you are *being* in unconditional love.

There is much that needs to change to alter the beliefs about sex that many on your planet hold. Sex is a pleasurable experience that one is intended to fully practice as a loving and respected part of your human existence. Shame and guilt were never intended outcomes of this wonderful experience. Please look to find a way to associate the feelings of love, honor, respect, joy, and excitement with sex instead of all the negative emotions that your societies place on it today. You and your planet will be the better for having let go of all the negative beliefs about sex.

Gay and Lesbian Relationships in Oneness

There is much negativity around same-sex relationships on your planet. Many of you believe gay and lesbian relationships are considered abhorrent, abnormal, and a sin. Those who participate in these relationships are made to feel guilt and shame, and are frequently outcast by their families and friends. Many of your religions have rules against these relationships and believe that they are against God's laws. God loves gays and lesbians exactly the same as he loves everyone else. There are no distinctions in God's unconditional love.

Judging someone for this type of behavior is as far from showing unconditional love toward your fellow brothers and sisters that a religion or person can be. Please stop persecuting these beautiful and loving children of God who are an extension of you. Being gay or lesbian is a very normal process within reincarnation and should never be considered abnormal. Everyone has been both at one time or another in their many lifetimes. It most frequently occurs when a being switches genders from one lifetime to the next and brings forward their physical attractions from their previous lifetime. Or in some occasions these individuals are playing out this experience as part of a planned spiritual learning, healing, or karma clearing. In some cases one can learn certain lessons only from having a same-sex partner.

These beautiful individuals are living exactly as was intended for them in this incarnation and are no different from any other being on your planet in their quest to experience all that they can while they are here in this lifetime. Look upon them with love and acceptance as you remember that there is a very high likelihood that you too have experienced many lifetimes of being gay or lesbian in your past experiences here on Earth. It is a natural process of transition from one lifetime to the next and needs no stigma attached to it. This way of *being* should be as accepted as blue eyes versus brown eyes versus green eyes. There shouldn't be any judgment attached to it whatsoever.

Blending Male and Female Energies in Oneness

So far in your human existence on your planet both sexes have equally manifested with the unique characteristics that would enable them to complete their life's purpose. Your innate talent and characteristics are intentional, meant to be used to accomplish your purpose, and are not gender specific. It was never intended for you to have exclusive or specific male or female gender roles, other than females giving birth. There are a few exceptions. In your history, men's physical strength made it natural to place them in roles that used their strength for protection, farming, building, and so on. But as your planet has become industrialized and now uses machines to perform many of these services, men's natural strength is no longer a major factor in survival.

As a continuation of your historical models created by your egoic thought systems, you have become fixated upon assigning traditional roles for males and females, which hasn't allowed for either sex to express their true selves. Each of you has been given innate talents, gifts, and characteristics to help you complete your life's purpose. For many of you these talents lie dormant or suppressed because they don't match up to what your societies consider appropriate for traditional male or female roles. Unfortunately, many of you have ended up leading lives of silent desperation and feeling unfulfilled because you haven't been allowed to *be* who you really are. As you quiet your egoic thought system and allow for the natural blending of your male and female essence, which is present in each of you, you will easily live in mutual respect and harmony with each other.

As your world shifts from living through egoic thoughts to living spiritually, your ways of living will change as well. The traditional roles for males and females will eventually cease to exist, and you will enjoy great love and harmony in your families, communities, and nation. Each person is in truth a blend of both male and female essence, which can enable him or her to live authentically on a daily basis. You can mindfully choose to maintain balance in your life so that you can better enjoy your new way of being. It is when one essence dominates the thoughts and behavior of a person that problems begin to occur. As an example, consider aggressive behavior, which is considered an extreme male essence. It is typically used in an emergency situation as a protection mechanism. Extreme behaviors are not intended to be continued past the point where they are needed in any given situation. Once the situation is over, your male/female balance would be regained through more loving and nurturing behavior.

The blending of the male and female energies can be
visualized as a pendulum with pure male energy at the
highest point on the right side of the body and the pure female
energy on the highest left side of the body. The male essence
is associated with logic and rational, linear thinking, whereas
the female essence is associated with feelings, caring,
nurturing, and compassion. To be in male/female balance the
pendulum would be centered at midpoint, where love, peace,
and unity consciousness resides. No matter which sex you are,
love, peace, and unity are the states you want to achieve to be
in male/female balance. Through love you achieve peace and
unity. Without love there can *be* no peace or unity.

You are intended to live your life through your feelings while
living your purpose in the *now*. Whenever one's essence
is out of balance, they are either too much into their mind
and not *being* in the moment, or too much into the moment
emotionally to gain the proper perspective on what is really
occurring in the now. Life is an inner journey of introspection
and spiritual growth, which manifests within the relationships
you have throughout your lifetime. It is in these relationships
that you come to know who you are and how you wish to *be*
in the *now* moments of your life.

In your new energy world, each child will be born knowing
his or her life's purpose. They will intuitively understand that
they also have the knowledge, talents, and characteristics to
be successful in their life's purpose. They will act according
to their spirit guides, using their natural talents and tendencies
in walking their path. Traditional male and female role
models will melt away and make room for the true essence of
each person to appear as intended. It will be the responsibility
of the parents, teachers, and their community to nurture and
support each child in their chosen life experiences.

Some beings may choose to forget who they really are or their
purpose for being here as an option of free will. However,
most of you will choose to know and grow to understand the
universal laws. Those who do not know who they are as a
child of God will live out their new life's purpose as someone
who is unaware, and that will be precisely as it should be. As
has always been true for your entire history on this planet,

everyone shows up exactly as intended in every moment of every day. This is true today and will be true tomorrow.

The blending of male/female essence can occur rather easily. It occurs in the absence of egoic thoughts. It entails living from your heart, with love and joy in all thoughts, words, and actions. It is constantly asking your spirit self, "What is the most loving thought, word, or action I can do at this moment?" until it becomes second nature to you. When you have arrived at that place, then you are acting out of love, peace, and Oneness, and your essence is in balance.

Male and Female Energies in Advanced Societies

In advanced societies both males and females are looked upon as equal. There are no thoughts or beliefs that one person is better than another in any way. Each person is recognized as having individual gifts and talents that were given to them so that they may fully experience their purpose in this lifetime. Behaviors are not labeled as male or female, as there are no beliefs of that nature. There is a mutual respect and appreciation for one another as they go about their daily lives with no judgment or status given to what a person does. No single profession is deemed more important or held in higher esteem than another, as each being is viewed as presenting their gifts to the community in whatever manner they wish.

Each person in advanced societies is looked upon as a unique individuation of God. They are each aware that their talents and gifts are part of their plan for ascension. They also understand that each being living in the physical plane is there to advance spiritually, and there is a mutual respect for each other within that knowing. They are united in their love and honor for each other, knowing that each person made the decision to be there so that they could fully experience all that they planned to occur in this incarnation.

In advanced societies whenever a person becomes out of balance in their male/female essence, they take a break and meditate. In their meditation, they seek an understanding of what occurred and how best to heal any situation created as an outcome of their imbalance. They seek Divine input about what to do to help them stay in balance moving forward. No one is made to feel guilty for their transgression, because each knows that they too will have these experiences at some point in their path. There is a gentleness and respect for the learning that is obtained in the here and now for everyone, no matter how small.

To begin to bring Oneness into the core of your families you must understand the universal truth that you are connected to everyone and everything.

Chapter 11
Families in Oneness

Creating Oneness in Families

On Earth your family dynamics vary significantly
from country to country and subculture to subculture.
Unfortunately, although it is the women who are most in tune
with each person in their families, it is typically the man who
is considered the head of the household and makes all the
decisions for the family. In many cases, this is not conducive
to happy families, as so many men live their lives from
their egoic thought systems. If your world's ever-increasing
reliance on antidepressants and other drugs is an indicator,
then you have to agree that this egoic dynamic serves neither
the family as a whole nor the individuals very well.

Traditionally, men have been taught to hold back their
feelings and that to show their emotions isn't masculine.
Showing love is neither a male nor female trait, but a
universal imperative for your Divine soul. Your true self
cannot be anything other than love. It is not that men aren't
capable of living from their spirit self; most simply choose
to live through their egoic thought systems instead. They
are unable to show up to their families as equal, loving, and
nurturing caretakers. Developing the natural loving and
caring qualities within each of you will help your planet move
to the higher dimensions of Oneness. It is the blending of
your female and male essence that brings balance within each
person. Whenever you shut down an aspect of yourself, you
are out of balance with yourself and the universe. Accept both
your male and female aspects, as together they allow you to
live your life in harmony with all there is.

Throughout your history, women have typically been more
adept at leading the family. They bear the children, take

responsibility for their care, and can better relate to children as a whole than their male partners. Again, this is not a universal female trait, and men are fully capable of tapping into these innate, natural qualities. They simply haven't been living through them in their daily lives for a very long time. It is a choice that I would encourage each man and woman to accept moving forward, not only toward their families, but toward all those who show up in their daily lives.

The new energy coming into your planet will enable men to more easily choose to take on roles traditionally assigned to women. To begin to bring Oneness into the core of your families you must understand the universal truth that you are connected to everyone and everything. Within your connectedness what you do for one another you are doing for yourself. Understanding this truth will begin at infancy and will be kept in the forefront of all that your children learn moving forward. Live this way moving forward so that your children will not be confused and grow more deeply to understand their connectedness.

In Oneness, women will easily accept their power and rightful position in families, businesses, and governments. Men will understand that their egoic way of living has not truly served their families and begin to accept their responsibilities in daily family dynamics. Men will learn to lovingly *be* in the moment with their children. Many will emulate the unconditional love observed in their wives. In the blending of your energies all roles will be shared and embraced. Both men and women will nurture their families through their spirit-guided intuition and genuine caring for all the members of their family. It is a true cooperative effort for the betterment of all. There is an ebb and flow to family dynamics, with each member stepping up in a loving and nurturing way to *be* an active participant in their daily lives. Your children will benefit greatly by witnessing this cooperation in action. They will become the love they are intended to *be* in all nurturing family and learning environments.

For those families that are new to these concepts, this will take some practice. For those who are already on a spiritual path, these changes should flow rather naturally within your

progression toward the fourth and fifth dimensions. As
with most changes to your family dynamics, some of these
behaviors may seem awkward at first, but they will become
second nature as you practice them daily with love, fun, and
acceptance. In any situation you may find your family, ask
yourself the following question: "What is the most loving
thing I can do or say at this moment that will best serve
everyone involved?" Listen for the answer from your spirit
self and act accordingly. This answer will lead you down the
path of joy and happiness.

The Role of Men in Families

Historically men have typically played a disproportionate
role in families. Their focus has primarily been to provide for
their families, and little has changed in thousands of years.
This restrictive dynamic neither supports each man's purpose
nor lends itself to a balanced, loving, and nurturing family
life. It is important for each man to know and understand
their purpose for being here so that they may fully step into
that purpose. Your purpose always involves relationships with
other people or living beings. You are here to learn how to *be*
more loving and supportive in your relationships. When you
understand this is part of what you have come here to do, you
can joyfully embrace your Divine power as it guides you on
your spiritual path.

It is unfortunate that many men have not been trained to
be nurturing. Many of your men today are far too focused
on competition or climbing the corporate ladder or finding
the next new discovery to notice they might have a more
expanded purpose than what they are currently doing. Your
life on this planet is all about your experiences with others and
how best to imitate Divine Love in these relationships. If you
have sequestered yourself away from others to do work, then
you are missing out on many of the experiences you wished
to have in this lifetime. Please be aware that this is not a trait
that is exclusive to men. Some women fall into this category
as well. Again, there is nothing wrong with this behavior; it
merely keeps you from experiencing all that you wished to
complete in this lifetime. It is always a matter of choice.

Maintaining balance in your life will become very important and allow you to have the experiences you wished to play out in this lifetime. Before coming down to Earth, you worked with your spirit guides to plan out major events that would occur in your life and the experiences you wished to have. Many of these experiences were planned to be played out in your family unit. Perhaps you wanted to learn to be a loving father of a gay child and to help that child grow up in an accepting and loving family environment. Or maybe you wanted to experience forgiveness for a spouse who had an affair and then go on to learn how to heal the relationship and make it stronger with greater love and understanding. Your part in learning from these types of experiences might be how to stay committed in a family relationship and working it out in a more loving and healing way. The balancing of relationships will more easily occur, as separate interests will no longer be the focus. Each person in the relationship will experience great joy, because all their actions are coming from love.

Each person must step back and consider the price paid by doing things that don't matter in the bigger picture of "you" on your vast soul journey. They will take the time to consider how they show up to others and what these relationships have to offer for learning love and spiritual growth. Men will become observers and eager learners of how to live more loving and nurturing in their relationships. They will show appreciation and gratitude for the gifts they have received, which will go a long way toward engendering love in their daily lives. Doing the little things in life will allow them to make someone's day easier and less stressful, which will also bring them more joy. They will check in with the Holy Spirit to guide them each day in how to be in the *now* moments of their day. They will begin to step back and ask themselves, "What is the most loving thing I can do at this moment?" More of them will also begin to ask what others would like to do and then bask in the fun of doing it with them.

There are no accidents in your life; all of the experiences that you have are there to serve a purpose in your spiritual growth. Remember to step back and ask your spirit self, "What does this event have to teach me? What is it that I wanted to experience and complete with this event?" It is in this asking that your answer will become known to you. Then thank the person who has played their part in your soul growth, as they agreed to play this part for your ascension. In most cases, your role in the experience has hastened their growth as well.

At this time I would like to ask you to please consider the personal damage that is done to others in your competitions. I know this is a social dynamic that has been a part of your history for thousands of years and is strongly entrenched into your daily lives. Nevertheless, I will now point out that within these games you physically hurt and damage others as a means of showing physical might in competitions. Let me repeat that: you physically hurt and damage others so that you can show physical might in games and competitions. You do this in a very big way, and yet you wonder why your society has broken down and you no longer care for one another.

You also train your children to play competitive games in which there must be a loser and a winner, and it is good only when you win. You buy your children games that teach them to kill others, they play these games for hours each day, and you wonder why they grow up to be aggressive, insensitive, or killers. What benefit is there in these rituals for your society? This is the egoic thought system at its height of insanity. Step back and consider these questions: Where you can personally make a big change in your family? Where can you make changes in your social dynamics?

There was a time in your history, perhaps in one of your past lives, when you lived as advanced beings and would have considered this type of behavior incomprehensible. Have fun and enjoy playing games, but not at the expense of others. This in no way resembles unconditional love. No one should be made to feel bad about their participation in a game or any other aspect of life. Perhaps you will consider not keeping score and just enjoy the event for the friendship, exercise, and joy of expression. Considering what benefits everyone who participates would allow you to have the right frame of mind for these events. In reality, no one is better than anyone else is, as you are all individuations of God. Each of you is here to express who you are, with the gifts and talents that will lead you to spiritual growth.

Please remember that as you work through your family
experiences, you are also teaching your children how best
to work out their own challenges and problems in a loving
and nurturing way. Your lives were not meant to be perfect.
They are meant to be an experience in learning how to show
up in a more loving and nurturing way in each relationship
that presents itself to you. It is by working through these
relationships that you will come to know deeper meaning
in your lives. Once you understand that true unconditional
love should be the primary focus in all relationships, you will
know greater joy and happiness in your lives.

The Role of Women in Families

Your egoic thought systems have placed many shackles onto
women so that you believe you must be the perfect wife
and mother and have the perfect job, perfect house, perfect
children, perfect furnishings, perfect car, or whatever else
perfect in order to be loved or successful. Please recognize
that this isn't being successful, nor will it bring you love. It
is a prescription for the total collapse of the core family, your
communities, and social consciousness. Things and titles
don't bring you success, love, or happiness. Joy comes from
giving unconditional love to others. Happiness comes from
the quality of the relationships in your life. Nurture these
and you will have all the love and joy that is slowly being
squeezed out of your commercialized lives. Please step back
to see what is really happening and make a conscious choice
to choose what will really bring peace and happiness back
into your lives. Once you have true peace back in your lives,
you will have so much joy that you will want to share it with
others.

The role of women in your families will not change much
in outer appearances in Oneness, except your lives will
slow down considerably. Throughout your history on Earth,
women have been the central point of love in most families.
Many have guided their families with unconditional love
and intuition, and have taught their children to embrace their
purpose. Others have not known unconditional love and were
unable to teach their children this powerful emotion or how

to pursue their life purpose. No one is wrong here, and no one is to be made guilty or judged. Many on your planet do not know the truth of their existence and were unable to teach what they did not know. Once you understand your role in relationships and can practice unconditional love with those you encounter, your life will change.

The challenge that most women need to overcome is the sacrificing of self for the family or job or both. When you are living from love, sacrifice disappears and love becomes your guide, and whatever task you are performing now becomes one of joy. To be true to who you really are, you must maintain balance in your daily life. You have a Divine purpose and need to step into it. Doing so allows your children to observe and learn how to maintain balance in their lives while still pursuing their purpose for being here. Look closely at your day and see where you can let go of false expectations and time commitments so that you may enjoy more mindful time with your family.

Please consider letting go of scheduling every moment of every day with senseless pursuits. Learn to sit in the quiet of your homes and turn inward to know who you really are. Invite your husband and children to meditate with you, so that they too can turn inward to know who they really are. Meditating as a family is a powerful tool for manifestation. It is also the path for peace, harmony, and love in your families. You are most likely already aware you will not find it in television, video games, sports, shopping, or owning things. Put your time into its optimum purpose and your life will flow in graceful harmony with the universe. Let the Holy Spirit guide your way.

Parenting in Oneness

The first step in parenting in Oneness is learning to *be* in the moment that is occurring *now*. Make the time each day to do morning and evening meditations together as a family. It will allow you to connect with the love and peace within you, as well as the universal Divine. You always have the option to choose what occurs in your day and how you are going to react to each event that occurs. *be* love in your thoughts, words, and actions and your children will emulate what they see occurring around them. Be positive in your thinking, as your thoughts are what manifest for you. Accept your power and lead your family on this path.

Once you have accepted Oneness and are practicing it throughout your day, you are ready to teach your children. Begin by teaching them the truth of who they are as children of God and that We are all family in our connectedness. Include in their lessons that they are each an individuation of God. Teach them to sit in the quiet of meditation so that they may hear their Divine inner voice and remember the truth of their existence. Their morning meditation can set the stage for a loving and joyous day for everyone they meet. Teach them to breathe deeply while they relax and let their minds go blank. Then tell them to listen for an inner voice that will talk to them and give them guidance. Help them recognize the difference between their spirit voice and their egoic voice. Their spirit voice is always loving and encouraging and wants them to do the right thing in all situations. Their egoic voice is demanding, impatient, and self-centered.

Raising a child in Oneness requires teaching them the truth of their existence and being a living example of how to *be* with others. In their early years, they will need to observe others living through unconditional love to fully understand the universal laws of connectedness and source. They will need to be reminded that their life energy is infinite and will live on forever. Understanding that they came to Earth in this lifetime to fulfill a spiritual purpose will help them seek their path and begin their journey as was intended for them. They need to connect to this knowledge to understand how to *be* unconditional Love in the *now* of each moment with everyone around them.

A major part of the responsibility of the parents and family in Oneness is to assist each child in their journey. This includes helping each person remember their origin and purpose, and to live from their spirit self. Remembering that they are a part of the love energy that is God will be the core principle in their understanding. Parents (plural) will also need to tap into their own spirit self to gain insight into what is the highest and best way to support each child on a daily basis. Each child is unique and has been given certain traits, gifts, and talents to support their purpose. As a parent, knowing how to best support and relate to them will bring more joy into your lives.

Nurturing Children in Oneness

Raising children in the knowledge they are a part of God and are connected to All That Is will open a new world of wonder for you as you watch them grow within their knowing. They will learn to use their natural abilities from birth moving forward. They will not have to relinquish the false beliefs that you have been taught. Children who are born now will be born with the innate knowledge of their existence. They will have retained the spiritual knowledge of their previous lives. Can you imagine the effect this will have on their lives for this generation and each subsequent one? Imagine the time, effort, struggle, and heartache that your children will avoid just by knowing these truths.

Teaching your children their truth and protecting them from adopting the false beliefs of the past will be a challenge for a period of time on your planet. Many of those who are unaware of who they are will shout from the rooftops their false beliefs and will want you to adhere to them. You will do well to remain diligent in speaking your truths while remaining patient and understanding of their position, as they are where you once were. Watch and learn from those who have become practiced at patience and understanding. Please remain loving and pure of heart as you traverse the many minefields of other beliefs. Surround them in love and hold their truth for them until they are ready to accept it for themselves.

As your planet adjusts to the fourth dimension and begins to move closer to the fifth dimension, more people will begin to awaken to the truth of their existence. There will be a tipping point in your future in which the process of awakening will accelerate faster and faster. It will be a time of great joy, as your lives will more fully reflect the love you have for your fellow brothers and sisters. This will allow your daily lives to play out in positive ways that you have not experienced on this planet for many millennia. All of the pain and suffering of your past will begin to melt away, and much joy and happiness will fill the air.

It is important that your children grow and learn in an environment that is loving and nurturing, where they are not considered bad or wrong. Explain to them that all boys and girls make mistakes and that it is a natural process of learning. And as your children learn, they will make mistakes, as that is all part of growing up. It is important that they understand that it is okay for parents to make mistakes, too, and that that is how parents learn. Make sure they know that everyone is loved no matter what mistakes they make. Teach them that mistakes can always be corrected by first stepping back to recognize that a mistake has been made, then reflecting upon what other choices were available to them, and then seeing which choice would have led them to the best desired outcome for everyone involved. Teach them to ask their spirit self the question, "What would have been the most loving thought, word, or action I can choose at this moment to obtain the highest and best outcome for everyone involved in this event?" Once they understand that each one of their thoughts, words, and actions affects others, they are on the right path toward understanding Oneness.

In my next book, I will address ways to teach your children about Oneness and how to maintain a balance between the two worlds of beliefs. It will also address acceptance for those who do not believe in the existence of a God or Divine Source. You will not be alone in your diligence to teach your children the truth of their spiritual and physical existence, and there will be many who will be able to assist you on this endeavor. It will take some time to develop, but seek out these new types of schools that will support your Divine truths. These schools will provide a place where children will be encouraged to use their spiritual gifts and grow to fulfill their purpose within your new fourth and fifth dimensions.

Teaching Children About Oneness

As mentioned earlier, children born into the world now will be born with innate knowledge. Unlike those born before them, they will retain the soul wisdom of their previous lifetimes. It is much like what occurs in the animal kingdom, where they instinctively know how to take care of themselves and function in the world. These new humans will know and understand Oneness and will even show up as your "teachers" in many areas. Be mindful to listen to them. As a parent, gently guide them in the direction of listening with their heart to their spirit selves. Fully support them in living through their emotions first, as this is the way of the future. Their intuitive knowledge will flow from their spirit self, and natural curiosity will prevail.

Work with your children to teach them how to feel their love and light and how to expand it to surround the world. Teach them to respect All That Is. Make sure your children learn to ask spiritual permission to engage others, human, or animal. They will want to gain permission before they observe, interact with, or care for others. Then further teach them to feel the responses to their requests in their heart and not their mind. Have them listen intuitively for their response. Ask them to role-play with each parent and sibling to experience the different feelings and the energy each of them emit. Practice with them so that they can feel and intuit the responses from you. Have them ask you for permission to do something verbally. Then intuitively send them either permission or denial. Practice doing both, so that they can learn to discern which feeling you are sending. Then have them practice with others in the family as well, because each person has their own subtle energy. Permission is a feeling of welcome and is accompanied by the feeling of inclusion and love. Denial of a request feels like resistance or pushing away. Then have them practice asking you questions through mental telepathy. This will hone both your intuition and theirs. Once you are in tune with each other's vibrations, begin to send them messages telepathically, so that you can grow these gifts in relationship to each other. From this work they will learn to respect each being's wishes and not enforce their will onto others.

Parenting in the new world will be a challenge for some time, as you are each learning new concepts and ways of *being*. It may be difficult at first to teach what you are just now learning. However, as you teach, you also learn, so don't be shy. Remember to make it playful so that it is a safe place to learn. Parents will need to remain diligent in spirit when answering children's questions. Step aside to let the Holy Spirit answer their questions for you. Then listen for the response that is best intended for each child at that time. It would not be in the child's best interest to learn a false belief or incorrect information that would later need to be unlearned. This will become much easier in time as you become more in tune with your spirit self and its connection to the Universal Divine Knowledge.

Families in Advanced Societies

Families in advanced societies create a core place where each person is safe to *be* who they really are and accepted at all times. Each person is appreciated for their role in their family and community. Your family becomes a place where mistakes are accepted and understood as a natural process of learning, healing, and spiritual growth. It is through your relationships that mistakes are corrected, relationships are mended, learning is accomplished, and karma is released. Love is ever present and reflected in all your interactions, and daily events play out in cooperation with each other. Each person has both a core and extended family, all of which lives in cooperation with his or her community and planet as a whole.

If you were to speak of family in an advanced society, you would need to be more specific about which family you are referring to. They would ask if you are referring to their core family or extended family or community family, as they consider themselves all family to each other. Their first thought of family would be their existence within the family of God. When speaking of their core family they would refer to their biological father, mother, sister, or brother. (Is it not easy now to see how a shift in one's beliefs ascends the universe?)

Families in advanced societies have different dynamics, depending upon whether or not they live in the country or in a large city. Those who live in the countryside live more simple lives, and they mingle and cooperate in their endeavors together. They tend to socialize more heavily within their core and extended families and with their close neighbors. In larger cities, life is more complex, with more mutual cooperation between people. They tend to specialize more in the roles they play and provide services to others who are frequently outside the family.

Most in advanced societies live in very close proximity to their biological families. Their extended biological family assists parents with raising their children, as well as with pooling of combined resources. They come together to assist each other in major events and daily chores, or rotate these responsibilities throughout the group. The roles each person plays in the family and extended family are cherished and appreciated. They know each person in relationship with them is a gift, and they treasure the time they have to spend with each other and the assistance each provides. If their biological family does not live near them, their community family assists them in a similar fashion.

In advanced societies, each person lives true to their passions in life. If someone loves to cook, then that is the role he or she plays in his or her family or community or both. Instead of each family cooking a separate meal, they may pool their resources to support eating their daily meals prepared by their family or community "chef." These types of arrangements allow the families to enjoy more time together without feeling stressed about all the things they need to accomplish. The pooling of their resources also serves to support those in their chosen path. The money they save in eating separately and the time they save in preparation goes to supporting those family members dedicated to working in the family unit, such as the family chef or home maintenance person.

Also in advanced societies, grandparents typically play a more significant role in raising grandchildren while their parents are working. The grandparents love, nurture, and teach the children during the day and then transition them to their parents after the evening meal. This is a major benefit to the family unit. They also know that the grandparents are far better equipped to raise children than their biological parents. These societies understand that the younger adults have not yet acquired the level of wisdom and experience needed to raise children with unconditional love and patience. Parents are very grateful for the opportunity to have their children loved and nurtured by their grandparents and appreciate the assistance. If grandparents are not available for this purpose, then the parents make similar arrangements within their community family. They seek out an older couple who are not yet blessed with grandchildren or live far away from their own children to fill this role for them.

Raising Children in Advanced Societies

Life is peaceful and serene for these societies. What they choose to do on a daily basis is looked upon within the bigger picture of who they are and what really matters. Their wants and needs are basic, as spending time with self and others is more precious to them than anything they could possibly own. They perform their daily activities from a place of love, so even the simplest tasks are given new meaning within the larger picture of their purpose for being here. There is a perpetual peace there that your world has not seen in many millennia.

Raising children in advanced societies is a community undertaking as well. They have the benefit of everyone knowing and supporting each other within their Universal Divine Knowledge of Oneness. Oneness is the common knowing that is interwoven into everything they think, say, or do. It is ever present in their governments, schools, businesses, and homes. From their earliest ages, children are taught that they are an individuation of Divine Source and that they are part of God and so is everyone else.

Teachers are groomed from childhood and guided to the subjects they will teach by their spirit selves. They know their purpose is to teach, and they are joyful in that pursuit. They are excited to be the guides for the next generation of talent that will bring forth new opportunities and products for their planet. The children are eager to learn, as they know what they are pursuing will allow them to fulfill their purpose. Parents, teachers, and members of their communities guide and assist each child on their path. They feel much joy when they are able to assist one another, and most extend their help whenever they are asked. It is important to note that help is given only when requested or permission is granted after an offer for help; to do otherwise would be considered a violation of personal power and could prevent spiritual growth. It could also create a karmic response from the universe. Protecting free will and obtaining permission before action are always in the forefront of their interactions.

Their children typically attend community schools and receive instruction in spiritual, social, and universal truths. They learn at their own pace, and their purpose guides them in the subjects they pursue. As part of their education, children learn the different dimensions of physical manifestation as well as the different dimensions of the nonphysical realms. They are connected to the Universal Divine Knowledge so they know in their core being that these teachings are truth. They also know that they have manifested in physical form in order to advance spiritually to a higher dimension. They know that they have been provided all the skills, traits, and talents they need to succeed. They know and understand the different cycles of reincarnation and how to advance spiritually from one dimension to another.

While they are young, they are taught the principles of intent and how it plays out in their lives. They grow to understand how the intent they project into their relationships directly correlates to the quality of their interactions with them. They also understand that they have a choice in the emotions they wish to experience in each moment of every day and how these emotions will define what occurs for them in their reality. They are lovingly coached through their daily real-life scenarios so they can step back and see what occurred and then see what other options were available to them to obtain their most desired outcome.

Curriculum in Advanced Societies

From their earliest ages children learn about their connectedness and the truth of who they are. Before they enter school, their early education is typically centered on learning to connect and live through their spirit selves. They learn to use and control their emotions to guide their actions. They learn that their feelings of joy emanate from love and their spirit self. They also learn that their negative emotions originate from their egos. They grow to understand how to determine if they are living from their egos or their spirit selves. Then they learn how to quickly shift to hearing their spirit voice once they realize they are operating out of their egos.

Once they are in school, they learn the principles of sacred geometry and how it relates to their physical world. These principles allow them to better understand the energies and correlations at work in the universe. From these principles, they gain relational knowledge of how the physical dimensions operate and how all is interconnected. They then learn of the nonphysical realm, how it has order and purpose. They understand that the physical and nonphysical realms are closely related, and that they can interact within both of them.

They are also taught the cycles of the universe, as well as planetary and dimensional evolution and ascension. They learn about their galaxy and those that are close by. They learn of the other physical planets and the societies on these planets. They understand that from this perspective they can learn about the technologies of their planet. Then they learn how these technologies operate within sacred geometry.

All children study and understand the cycles and orbits of their galaxy. They learn about their planet and their solar system, and how it interrelates with other galaxies. They also understand how the orbits of planets affect the energy around them. They learn the higher realms of consciousness and how they are all interrelated. They come to know how one could traverse these dimensions within their ascension plan. They become knowledgeable in how to attain and use the gifts that are available to them at the different levels of ascension and the responsibility that comes with these gifts.

They learn the universal laws and the consequences of not living them. They understand the principles of manifestation and how to incorporate them into their daily lives. They understand the responsibilities that these gifts bring with them. They are also taught how to heal their own bodies and create well-being for themselves and others. They are taught about their physical chakras and the energy meridians of their physical body. They learn how the energy of each chakra affects the neighboring organs of their body. They learn the correlation between illness and blocked energy centers or negative egoic thoughts. They learn techniques to clear blocked energy and help their bodies heal. As you can see, there is much that you have yet to learn, and all will be provided to you at the right timing for each person in their ascension plan.

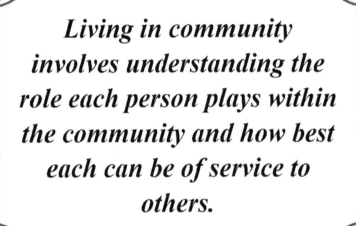

Living in community involves understanding the role each person plays within the community and how best each can be of service to others.

Chapter 12
Creating Oneness in Community

Stewardship in Community

Living in community involves understanding the role each person plays and the responsibilities created from being a member of a community. People more fully understood this in your recent past. Unfortunately, at this time, some of you have come to live by an each-man-for-himself mentality. Your lives have become commercialized with a constant bombardment of information. This constant pinging of frivolous stimuli has caused you to forget who you are and how to *be* within a spiritual life. Community is about interaction, harmony, cooperation, and Oneness. It is a place of peace and serenity.

Communities were initially created out of the need for protection. They have evolved into complex regions of multitalented individuals commingling with others to meet individual, family, and community needs. Most started out as family groups and then extended to include more and more individuals who could provide specialized services for the group. These groups have transformed themselves into huge cities where neighbors no longer know each other, and there is little sense of community and interrelatedness.

Your global community encompasses your planet, people, animals, natural resources, businesses, and government. It can become a global community where all are living in harmony with one another. This means making decisions on all levels of government and in businesses that provide for the highest and best outcome for all locally, nationally, and globally. You are all interconnected within the one body of Earth, which is contained within the Divine Universe of God. Would you not care for your hands or feet in order for your body to maintain complete health? Viewing your resources and all inhabitants on your planet as one body would help you make choices that are for the good of all.

It is also important to note here that contrary to what your laws seem to provide you, in reality, you are only temporary caretakers and stewards of your planet and do not own any part of it. This is an important concept for each of you to understand spiritually so that you can more readily assume your stewardship. Please step back to see the larger picture of your spiritual evolution and pause to remember the many visits you have already made to Earth. Now take pause again and consider the ones you will make in your future.

Since you will be here again, don't you want your planet to be a safe and healthy place to experience upon your return each time? Or do you wish to experience the pain and agony of a planet that is dying and can no longer sustain its inhabitants? Please consider that ensuring you have left your planet in a better state of being than when you arrived might very well be a part of what you wished to experience while here on Earth in this lifetime.

To ensure the highest and best good in mind for all beings on your planet, it would be an important step forward to ensure your planet reaches a global agreement to adopt the Divine universal laws as the basic principles for living on Earth. You cannot live in harmony with everyone without first understanding that you are all connected, and what one does in one country really does affect everyone else on your planet. The universal Divine laws are operating at all times in your universe, whether you believe them or not. With this in mind, wouldn't it make sense to acknowledge and globally adopt them into your daily lives?

Creating Oneness in Community

Oneness is a state of being, and as such, can be created only through the energy and vibrations of love. Moving away from the egoic thought system to live in the energy of love will take much work, but the rewards are greater than you can imagine. When you are living your life from Oneness, all that is around you becomes a reflection of your love. You cannot be anything else. The joy and happiness that you feel keeps this love within you, and you will begin to resonate from love to peace, to Oneness, back to love, to peace and Oneness again. It allows you to live your life in joy and happiness and in harmony with the All that Is that is God.

Living in Oneness means that you are in balance with everything that resides in your community. That includes all the resources, plants, and animals within your community and its span of control. I am referring not only to your local community, but to the community of God, the All That Is. You are an active participant in the ebb and flow of the energy of nature and all of those within your community, planet, and universe. Living within the Oneness community is a responsibility and commitment to harmonize with and protect everyone and everything within this space.

In advanced societies, everyone is equal and everyone is drawn to assist anyone who is lacking and wishes assistance. Everyone is provided a place to live, has food to eat, and has equal access to education and work if that is what they desire. They ensure that there are no areas of poverty in any community and that everyone is taken care of equally. They consider it their global responsibility to ensure that all are able to live with dignity and respect in their chosen area of pursuit. These are not perfect societies, and there are those whose purpose is to show contrast. Some of them do not live in Oneness and choose not to work or give to their communities. They are recognized as being there to provide contrast and are accepted in this role as part of their societies.

Igniting the Spark of Oneness

Love naturally wants to extend out and connect to others, and this is your natural state of *being*. Igniting the spark of Oneness within your new world begins within each person. Once you know and understand your Oneness, you will want to expand your love and light out into the world as you begin and end each day, as well as throughout your day. You will want to connect with others to plan out and provide for a better future for all within all your communities. You will begin to participate in your community meetings to learn where you can help. Then you will participate in planned events where your families can enjoy the teamwork of pursuing a goal together.

It would benefit you greatly if love and light were in the forefront of each interaction that you have with each other. Telepathically ask permission to engage with each person you come into contact with on a spirit level first, and then fully engage him or her from the love and light that is within you. Then interact with them on the physical plane from your spirit selves and see how different your interactions become. This is Oneness, loving, and respecting All That Is with joy and harmony.

Creating Oneness requires one to be fully engaged in what is occurring around them. One way to begin to create a spark of Oneness in your community is to volunteer to assist in existing programs or to start your own program to fill a need that is not being met. It is important to note that if it is not your calling, you are under no obligation whatsoever to do volunteer work and you may not feel like doing so. Do this work only if you feel it is something you would like to pursue, and check in with your spirit self to see if it is the right choice for you.

In order for you to stay in the frequency of love, you will need to ensure that you are nurturing and loving with yourself before you can begin to assist others. You will be unable to resonate in the frequency of love while you do this work if you are feeling overwhelmed or stressed or feel it is an obligation. Please be clear on this: there is no obligation to do anything here. If you are so inclined and are coming only from love, then please pursue this type of work. If not, then please be kind and loving toward yourself. Take care of yourself first. Do what is in your personal highest and best interest at all times. When the timing is right, then expand it to assist others.

If you feel motivated to assist others, begin by helping those who are closest to you in your families and neighborhoods, then expand your presence farther into the community. Ask those you have helped to "pay it forward" to others so that many more are brought into your new sense of community. Be the love that you are, and you will reflect that outward toward others. There are many things that you can consider to help others. Perhaps you will be called to bring a child into your home who doesn't have one, or you will feel called upon to work with the elderly to help them with projects they can no longer perform around their homes. Maybe you will consider using alternative methods to heal the sick and injured. Once you have been granted permission to help, form a group of family, friends, or neighbors to come together to assist you with your endeavors.

When you begin these projects, ensure that you are providing help where help is wanted. Don't assume someone will automatically want your help. If you are doing this in an organized fashion, then have them either subscribe to your services or fill out a form that describes what they would like you to do. Then do only what you have received permission to do. Perform high-quality workmanship that reflects the love, compassion, and happiness you feel while doing this work, and joy will abound for everyone involved. This is truly unconditional love at its best, giving without thought of anything but the love that is behind the giving.

Take one weekend a month to do these projects. See if your company will sponsor you in this endeavor and allow you one day off a month or quarter in order to do them. Show your company the work you are doing and how you are affecting the lives of those around you. Encourage others to begin similar groups within their families, groups of friends, and neighborhoods. Stage a block party after each event and encourage as many neighbors and friends as possible to attend. Find out who else needs assistance, and enlist others to become part of this movement. The love that will be present at these events will have an immense impact on your lives.

Some of you will begin to expand this program to include your nursing homes, hospitals, schools, parks, and public spaces. As others participate in these projects and programs, they will want to step into their power to assist in the areas

where they have a specific interest. All it takes to begin
a community movement like this is to ignite a spark of
unconditional love within yourself, and then expand it to
others, who will also feel the love and joy that comes from
being in true community.

The love, joy, and happiness you will gain by helping others
will feel wonderful. You will also start new friendships
along the way, which will be an added benefit for all parties
involved. Remember, you don't have to do any of these
projects. You are here to do what brings you joy and serves
your purpose. Do exactly that with love and joy in your heart,
and you are exactly where you are supposed to be.

Governmental Services in Oneness

In advanced societies governmental services are offered to
help each community provide for the basic needs of all those
living within its boundaries. These services are fairly basic
and usually include housing, transportation, food, clothing,
health care, education, spiritual counseling, and protection.
Each society provides the services deemed most appropriate
for their planet, climate, state of spirituality, and physical
being.

Community leaders are elected from a group of qualified
candidates who have been specifically educated and trained
to be civic leaders. This is their purpose. They rule by elected
councils who are made up of individuals coming from
different talents and specialties so that they may provide
recommendations to the council in their areas of expertise.
Decisions are made by majority vote and carried out by the
appropriate departments of each branch of government.
They lead from their guided spirit selves and always have the
highest and best outcome for all in the forefront of each of
their decisions.

Advanced societies understand that they are merely stewards
of their planets and don't own any land. They may, however,
rent or own homes or buildings. When one becomes an adult,
they can choose to either remain in their family home or apply

for and receive a home of their own. Their homes are small, as they value nature and they would not want their community presence to affect their natural surroundings.

Their homes in rural areas are small and spaced within open areas of shared land and resources. These resources include parks, recreational areas, farmland, and community centers. They live close to where they work, and travel via shared resources as well. Those living on higher-dimensional planets merely think of where they want to go and are immediately teleported there.

In many advanced societies, those who live in large communities choose to build multifloor buildings so that their impact on nature and the land is minimal. Again, their homes are very small and are allocated according to the size of their family and proximity to their work. They strive to maintain green areas around all buildings so that they can still enjoy nature and commune in the outdoors. Many communities also provide their citizens with utilities and public transportation.

Although crime is fairly rare in higher-dimensional realms, most communities also provide police and security services. Their facilities and police forces are relatively small, and they may provide other community services in addition to protection. At times there are those who choose to disobey laws, and they are dealt with according to the laws of their community. Those who disobey laws are typically brought before a legal tribunal to determine their crime, if any. Then they are tried in front of a tribunal, and if found guilty, they live the associated consequences.

Health Care in Oneness

Health care in Oneness will look different for you in the near future. Your services will include healing modalities that provide for balancing your Divine energy and working to resolve past life and current life conflict and any distortions that have caused illness. Your counseling services will include working with individuals to understand the truth of their existence and their connectedness to the All That Is.

These services will also include working with patients to help them understand their egoic thought system. Once they have an understanding, they can learn how to move past it into higher-consciousness thinking through their spirit selves.

As you take on healing the source of your illnesses through energy work, your health care services will shift from treating the symptoms of your illnesses to teaching people how to heal themselves. Your health services will expand to include sound, light, and touch healing modalities. There is much for you to learn about how your thoughts, words, and actions can manifest to create disease in your bodies. There are many spiritual healers on your planet to help you learn all that you can about your true selves. Once you understand that you create the origin of illness, you can begin to heal yourselves and others.

Most advanced societies have the ability to heal themselves, so a large health care system is not necessary on those planets. Health care services are provided free of charge by their communities on a much smaller scale. They know and understand that whenever an individual is having a health issue, it typically is the result of an imbalance in their spiritual energy centers. When they are treated for any energy center problems, the associated physical problems usually disappear rather quickly. Where the problem has been long term or the damage more pronounced, they then seek assistance from healers or physicians.

Their medicine is geared more toward treating injuries than illnesses. Unlike your medical care, they treat the cause of illness at the source of the illness. Illness is an outcome of self-deprecating negative thoughts and feelings. They know it is best treated with a combination of spiritual counseling, herbs, massage, and energy healing modalities. Physicians are not usually involved unless the patient has allowed the situation to become critical. Most patients seek assistance for energy imbalances as soon as they begin to feel out of sorts. By seeking care early, diseases are easily stopped at their originating site, and the distortion dissolves.

Advanced societies don't have the end-of-life experiences
you do on your planet. When one has completed all that they
wished to complete or is severely injured or has a debilitating
disease, they choose to lay their body down and continue on
to their next plane of existence. Their families and friends
understand this choice and know that their loved ones are
still available to them even though they have moved on to
their next dimensional experience. Although their families
and friends are saddened and miss the presence of their loved
one, they understand each person's choice to move on to their
next experience. When one chooses to lay their body down,
they typically gather their family and friends to announce
their decision so that they will have sufficient time to say their
good-byes. They most typically do this before their quality of
life is degraded, as they do not want to become a burden upon
their families or community. There is a peace and serenity
around the passing of a loved one, and they are given a loving
send-off to their next endeavor.

Businesses in Oneness

Moving your planet away from greed, control, and profits
may take many years but will eventually occur. As you
mature spiritually and move toward the fifth dimension, your
views on ownership, profits, and control will soften, and you
will begin to understand your true roles in society. When
businesses are operating in Oneness, they provide services
and goods at a reasonable rate and with limited profits. They
do it with integrity and always with the highest and best good
for their planet, community, and customers in mind. They
see themselves as temporary guests of the planet and wish
to leave the planet in a better state than when they arrived
so that those who follow will be able to fully enjoy their
experiences as well.

Businesses in Oneness are typically found at more local or
regional levels to best serve those around them and allow
for the distribution of wealth to all regions of the planet. The
businesses employ and support local talent in their purposes.
Workers are placed into jobs only where they have a passion
for the work they will be doing; to do otherwise would not

serve the individual, the business, or the community. The goal of all in Oneness is to ensure that everyone enjoys what they are doing so that the highest level of joy and love is ever present. This attention to service helps to maintain high spiritual energy levels for the individual, business, and community.

Within Oneness, profits are reasonable and capped so that customers pay reasonable prices for their goods and services. Excess profits are gladly given to the charity of choice by each company to be used to assist communities and those who are in need. When profits are too high, prices for the goods are lowered accordingly. Those who own and lead companies understand that they are only stewards of these businesses and that part of their role is to assist others in their pursuit of spiritual growth and purpose in this lifetime. They run their businesses with the joy of knowing the goods and services they provide to their communities are also fulfilling the purpose of their employees within Oneness.

Within the higher-dimensional advanced societies, all is owned by the All. They know their connectedness and share everything equally. Everyone provides a service to the community, and the community services everyone. Their intent is to use only what they need and replace all that they are able to replace. All natural resources are protected and not over allocated. Where resources or goods are found in only one region, the inhabitants of that area take it upon themselves to ensure that the resources are made available to all those in need around the planet on an equal basis. Protecting the planet is of the utmost importance to them, and they take this responsibility seriously. They have the same view of other planets and their resources as well.

Monetary System in Oneness

Currently on your planet, money appears to be the root of all greed and plays a role in most of the power struggles in your societies. In truth, it is merely a symbol of what you value and the means by which you obtain what you desire. For some of you, your current social mores and personal interactions play out in such a way that acquiring material objects is a status symbol, and you use these rank standards as a means to define yourselves.

We observe many of you wanting, wanting, and wanting more. Some seem so desperate that they acquire more than they could possibly ever use. There are those who feel they are lacking unless they can validate that they own more than others. When they deem they have more, they pronounce themselves happy. But are they really? Maybe, until they see someone else who has more, and then they lose their sense of self once again and must amass more to bolster their self-esteem. There is nothing wrong with living this way, and it is always an option, but can you see the madness in this game they play with themselves?

As mentioned earlier, neither money nor the goods it buys can provide you with the love and happiness that each of you desperately hungers for in your lives. Love and happiness can come only from within you and are the direct result of living a life of loving intent in all that you do and being of service to others. Having a loving intention for the money that you spend will also create a space for love, honor, and compassion in its spending and allow for continued manifesting of it in the future.

As you move closer to the fifth dimension, your views of money and the role it plays in your life will change. The significance you place on money will soften, and you will begin to make more conscious choices in how you use it in your daily lives. This softening will come as a direct outcome of your understanding how to lovingly manifest in your life. You will find that your true needs can be met through other avenues of your life, as your relationships will become more important to you. And any cravings to own more than you need will have been quieted in the process.

In advanced societies there are no monetary systems. They have devised a system of exchanging goods for goods, services for goods, and services for services to meet their needs. There is no need for hoarding, for they lack nothing. All of their basic needs are met within their societies, and if they so choose, they can always acquire specialty goods or services as they wish through additional exchanges of services or goods they have acquired.

Military in Oneness

Your planet has governed from a position of strong military power centers for thousands of years. You derive your sense of security from knowing that if need be, you can force others to adhere to your standards of social order and structure. There is no one to make wrong here. It is just an outcome of the fear that is prevalent on your planet at this time. In your fear of the loss of resources, power, and freedoms, you give your governments and military much leeway to amass weapons and act out in times of strife and unrest. Be aware that it may very well be your own freedoms they ultimately reduce in the name of keeping peace. Be diligent so that this does not occur.

Maintaining a delicate balance of love, peace, and harmony will continue to be a challenge for some countries while you transition from a third- to a fourth-, and then a fifth-dimensional planet. A few countries will remain challenged by their prejudices and religious views of the world. As with everything in the spiritual realm, the actual intent of the action plays the most important role in the outcome of any event. If you have pure intent of protection and preservation of freedoms for everyone, then the military has a purpose in Oneness. If a military regime is used for the "protection" of a country and it is done out of hate, prejudice, or greed, then the outcome will be far different for those who participated in the actions.

As a result of public pressure, many countries will naturally move to reduce the size of their military as an outcome of knowing Oneness. Arsenals of weapons will be reduced, and budgets will be reallocated to make way for opportunities to help those in need and heal your planet. How quickly this occurs is dependent upon how rapidly the Divine universal laws are approved and adopted by each country. This will also be initiated and established through public pressure. Those countries that do adopt the universal laws will naturally move away from being a fear-dominated society to being one of love, peace, and harmony. These Oneness countries will emerge as the benefactors of the intent and goodwill they send out as they help their neighboring brothers and sisters. As they send out their help to others, it will be returned to them many times over as their neighbors are able to begin to help themselves in their new Oneness. These countries new to Oneness will then begin to reflect and send back the love, peace, and harmony that were offered to them. It is in the process where you will see the turning wheel of Oneness making its presence known throughout the world.

In advanced societies, the military is small and typically needed only when there are large groups operating out of their egoic thought system and wishing to force their will onto others. This does not occur very often and most typically only on those planets in lower-dimensional realms. Because the need of military forces is rare, these forces are most typically used for humanitarian and natural disaster recovery scenarios. In the higher-dimensional planets, the military is operational at a planetary level and managed by their global council. It is a concept similar to the original establishment of the United States of America, but more along the lines of a United Countries of Earth evolution.

Assistance with Oneness

There is much that must be accomplished on your planet, and changing beliefs about who you are and understanding what your role is while you are here is the first step. This is the most important step, as it requires you to shake the foundations of what you have learned until now in this and previous lifetimes. It also requires you to replace these beliefs with new concepts that require greater faith than you have had to experience in many lifetimes. In truth, you have been the keepers of the light of Oneness for thousands of years, and We ask that you continue to steer the course toward Oneness. Your rewards will be great, and your joy will resonate around the globe. You are at the cusp of a great adventure that will bring your planet back into balance with the universe.

We are here to assist in your ascension and have placed many masters, healers, and teachers amongst you now. Seek them out to assist with personal, social, and political changes that will start the momentum going in the healing direction. We also ask that you please consider setting aside your materialism and choosing another path that supports the healing of your planet. To move forward in your ascension, you may choose to become the change agents many of you are intended to be and begin a movement of transformation, which will bring your planet, lives, communities, governments, and businesses back into spiritual balance. Keep moving forward, no matter how small the change you make. Take the time to celebrate each change that you do make. It all matters. Begin to make any changes first within your families and then expand them to your local communities. At the same time, look at electing and supporting local, state, and national leaders who can support your spiritual awakening and Oneness movements into the fifth dimension.

Doors will open for you when you are at the right moment for change. Opportunities will present themselves to you. Look for them, and step into your role for these events. Check in with your spirit self to find out what actions are of the highest and best good for you to do each day. In this asking, your opportunities will be made known to you. We love and honor you with much gratitude for the work you are doing. We experience great joy as We watch you expand who you are and accept the opportunities that are presented to you. You are never alone, and We are eager to help. We are only a thought away from you in any moment.

Earth in Oneness

Eventually your planet will evolve to become a single nation united in Oneness called Earth. When Oneness is all that you are and can be, you will be ready to interact cooperatively with your neighboring planets. But first, you must learn to crawl, then walk, and then run, as you like to say on your planet. This spiritual and legal unification of all your nations under God, indivisible in your Oneness, with liberty and justice for all, will need to be taken forward one step at a time. For now, bask in the knowledge that you will someday have evolved to the spiritual level where you can travel to see and interact with your extended families on other planets. This can take a long time to occur or can be done in a short period of time. It will occur as an outcome of your planet having reached the appropriate level of ascension into Oneness and accepted the responsibilities of communing fully in unconditional love. This is now and has always been part of Earth's plan.

Your interplanetary contact will take place on Earth first, as others are from more advanced societies and can travel with ease. Many of them will come to teach those who are ready to learn and have reached an appropriate level of spiritual evolution to be able to understand what they have to teach. They are delighted with your ascension. They are making themselves readily available to teach you how best to live in Oneness. They can also assist you with developing new technologies to sustain your planet. They will come from the same planets you left thousands of years ago. They have been living in Oneness for thousands of years and have assisted other planets with their ascension as well. There is much joy and excitement as they await your acceptance of their wish to assist. Your acceptance of their offer will make it so.

Accepting these universal laws will allow all religions to become facilitators for spiritual and social ascension. What a glorious gift of unity in Oneness religions can give their followers.

Chapter 13
Oneness in Worship

Commonality of Religions

Most of the religions on your planet have a core belief in a
supreme being, and that there is a higher plane of existence.
Many believe in the concepts of living a life that is free from
negative influence, and that each person should be treated
as one would like to be treated. Where they diverge is in the
names they call their gods and within their rules and beliefs
of how their followers should live their lives. Living in
Oneness will enable all religions to discard erroneous beliefs
and rules that do not foster Oneness and move their purpose
toward accepting the universal Divine laws. Accepting these
laws will allow all religions to become loving facilitators for
spiritual and social ascension. What a glorious gift of unity in
Oneness religions can give their followers.

Understanding Oneness will become the catalyst for change
in all religions. Again, there is no intent here to make any
religion wrong or more correct than any other. There is no
need to abandon your religions. All paths lead to God. We
have already discussed the beliefs that religions and societies
as a whole would do well to discard in order to support each
person's purpose for being here on Earth. These changes in
core beliefs will need to occur for your planet to advance to
its next level of ascension. Some religions will embrace these
changes and others will not at this time, and that is what is
right for them now. Each person is ascending at his or her
own rate. Each must decide what beliefs resonate within their
soul for them at this time.

Religious leaders are here at this wonderful time to help
your planet move from a third-, to a fourth-, and then to a
fifth-dimensional plane. The truth of your existence must

be understood, accepted, and internalized to move you forward. Many of your followers are awakening to this truth on a daily basis. As more and more of them are awakened in the near future, there will be a tipping point of universal knowledge that will cause most on your planet to become fully awakened. That will be a wonderful and glorious day for your planet. You have waited a long time for this to occur, and We rejoice with every heart that is opened to the love and light of your truth.

There Must Be Another Way

The days of pointing a finger at one another and saying that only one religion is correct and the others are wrong are gone. In reality, all religions began with the truth of your existence. You are all individuations of God, interconnected in your Oneness, and indivisible in your glory. Religions that are now awakening to the truth of their Oneness will be able to more quickly understand the role they can play in your lives moving forward. To accept their intended roles at this time, religious leaders will need to understand the ascension process and how best to serve those in need.

The ascension process does not have to be complex. It involves discarding those beliefs that do not support the truth of your existence and replacing them with the truth. Although it may not be complex, it can be a difficult task for many who have held fast to their beliefs and are inflexible to hearing their truth. Religions must first consider that there is something they do not currently remember about God that when known again will change their views of God and the universe. It means setting aside egoic prejudice and pride and reaching out to welcome God's light of truth into your consciousness. It means turning inward on a personal spiritual level first, to remember your truth and purpose for being here. Once you remember who you are, We ask that you step back into your roles as religious leaders to serve your congregations during their ascension toward Oneness.

We have sent you many masters, and they are available to assist you within your many religions. Seek them out and help them be the change agents that will lead all to the truth. Many of your followers are awakening at this time and would benefit greatly from hearing the truth from their religious leaders. If they cannot find it there, they will seek it out in other places. It is always a choice in how you lead your religions. Please remember that it is the intentions of your thoughts, words, and deeds that will determine the ultimate outcome. Choose your thoughts, words, and deeds wisely, and lead from love and Oneness, and your outcomes will bring you great joy.

Assisting your congregation in the ascension process is the need your religions can fill at this time. It is important to stress that your assistance must include the full truth of what is occurring and not half-truths. Your assistance is greatly needed in teaching everyone how to release the egoic thought system so that each person can learn to live from his or her spirit self. *A Course in Miracles* has been translated into many languages. It is making its way around the globe. Use it as the tool it was intended to be. Understand and learn from it, as releasing the ego is an essential step in the ascension process. Seek out those who have been students of the *Course* and incorporate their learning into your teachings.

We respectfully request all religious leaders to step back and reflect on the bigger picture of your spiritual journey into infinity. We ask you to imagine that within this tiny speck of time you have the potential to make a huge contribution of collaboration and change that will lead to the ascension of your planet to a higher spiritual realm. What a tremendous feat you can accomplish in coming together at this amazing time here on Earth. Remember what We said earlier, that every person on your planet today is here to assist in this ascension. Your purpose is to help others in this process. With much excitement and anticipation, We ask you to step into your purpose now and accept it with joy and love. Your life will be the better for it, and you will rejoice in the happiness that living your purpose will bring.

Although We make these requests on a global level, We also ask each of you who are a part of organized religion who are reading this to consider reaching out and letting your awakening be known to others. Check in with your spirit self to know when the timing is right for you to do this and with whom. Remember that when the student is ready, the teacher will appear. Seek out those who are of similar awakening, and learn your truth. You will know it is your truth when it resonates in the depth of your being and you want to shout it out to everyone. Become the new champions of change within your religions.

Pulling Religions Together

The core of all religions is the desire to live in Oneness. As mentioned earlier, it would be an important major step forward for your planet to reach a global agreement for everyone to adopt the Divine universal laws. Acceptance and adoption can occur much sooner if it is supported and advocated through religious leaders initially. Religions can choose to fully recognize and accept their spiritual truth between and amongst themselves first. Once the Divine universal laws are adopted and practiced within religions, the countries of your planet can more fully accept their spiritual role in the Divine Universal Sonship. Put another way, a global spiritual awakening should occur first before the world will be ready to unite to make changes at a governmental and planetary level.

Many religious leaders in your world will choose to sponsor a global initiative to unite all religions to support the truth of your existence. This initiative to support the Divine Universal laws would replace sections of current erroneous religious doctrines with the truth of your existence. Seek out the enlightened masters amongst your religions to learn your role in the new way of *being*. They are beginning to make themselves known to you. Also take the time to turn inward to hear the Holy Spirit through your spirit selves. Learn and then teach the Divine universal laws that are always operating whether or not you currently believe or know of them. You will be far better off for having made the effort. Remember that you will feel joy as an outcome of your loving actions and fear as an outcome of your egoic actions. Use your emotions to guide your way.

Your new doctrines can allow your religions to practice within a new framework that depicts God and his Sonship as they truly are. This transformation will allow all religious followers to accept their place in the Universal Sonship and begin to understand their roles in Oneness. There is much work to be accomplished to bring your planet back into harmony and balance. If religions so choose, they can begin to play a pivotal role in helping the nations of the world accomplish ascension while maintaining peace and harmony. We wait in joyous anticipation to observe your unification within the Divine truth. The truth is that each of you is an individuation of God, united in Oneness and indivisible in your glory."

Religions in Oneness

Religions are intended to support individuals on their spiritual path. Oneness in religions can best be expressed through supporting and teaching the personification of God's expression of love toward everyone. In learning these teachings, each person becomes that love for all who walk the path along with them. Religions in Oneness are a place where one can go to hear the truth of their existence and gain wisdom while learning from masters.

Understanding how the ego operates in your daily lives requires you to recognize how it controls out of fear and keeps you from the love that is your inheritance. Teaching the principles of *A Course in Miracles* can become a means of reunifying your congregations and servicing their need for knowledge and understanding, and providing the tools to support their new way of *being*. Although it is not the only tool that can be used for this purpose, it is one of the most complete and comprehensive ones available today. Please consider using it as your foundation of truth; it can lead you and your congregations to understand the forces that are at work in the universe at this time. There is much to be accomplished, and there is a hunger for the truth.

Once your followers have learned that fear is the opposite to love, that We are all connected in our individuation of God, and that they are equally loved by God, they will be well on their way to knowing Oneness. There is much work to do to become religions within Oneness. It is not an insurmountable task. Each and every small step is important. Set aside all your fears and give them to God. Allow him to assist you in your process of change. Your religions will be all the better for having done so. With much love and honor We gratefully watch as you progress through the stages of change and ascension.

Leadership in Oneness is a beautiful symphony played out between quality laws, social services, and the distribution of resources amongst all people of Earth.

Chapter 14
Leadership in Oneness

Leadership in Oneness

Leadership in Oneness is a beautiful symphony played out between universal humanitarian laws, social services, infrastructure, and the balanced distribution of resources amongst all people of the community, nation, and planet. It is the ability to maintain this delicate balance that provides leaders the continued support of their constituents. There are no special interests in Oneness. All interactions are organized and acted upon from the perspective of what is of the highest and best good for all. It is extremely rare, but if a leader chooses to put special interests ahead of the highest and best good for all, that is reason to remove that leader from office.

In advanced societies, galactic leaders are elected from an approved list of educated, trained, and experienced business and civic leaders. These leaders are groomed and trained from an early age to be leaders. It is their purpose for being on the planet. They may also choose to enter the public leadership arena through the path of business management. From there they obtain additional education and training before their names are placed on the list of approved leadership candidates. They begin their careers by being elected at the community level, and then advance to lead larger communities at a regional or state level, then a national level, and finally at the galactic level.

Only a few leaders are called upon to lead at the galactic level. Leading at the Galactic Council level requires understanding multidimensional planets and their unique challenges. Having extensive knowledge of planets, their dimensions, universal laws, sacred geometry, resources, and unique planetary challenges is required before being able to discuss assistance, interactions, and future planning between the planets. It is important that more highly evolved planets not interfere with the procession of learning and advancement taking place at the lower spiritual levels. They would not want to create a situation where spiritual growth is stymied because of interference. Expressing free will and advancement in spiritual growth are the core intentions for physically manifesting, and to interfere with these processes could cause karmic repercussions. That is why the Divine universe requires you to request help before giving it.

The Role of Women in Leadership

After many millennia of male dominance on your planet, the pendulum is swinging in the direction of a world led by women, who will bring your planet back into balance, harmony, and peace. This will occur so that the world can be ruled from a place of mutual cooperation, honor, and respect. When all parties involved in the leadership-decision process know and understand the value of honor, compassion, trust, and love, your world can move into an extended period of stabilization and peace. Once the world is stabilized and living through mutual cooperation, honor, and respect, you will be ready to move to the next level of evolution.

In the beginning of your history, women were the leaders of all communities. They led through their highly-evolved spiritual connections to the Divine, nature, and all beings around them. These women ruled as a group of spiritual leaders with mutual cooperation and honor. They understood the importance of looking at the whole picture and choosing solutions to problems that were in the best interest of all involved and their impact on nature. They viewed sustainability of their societies and environments with the greatest importance so that their communities could continue to thrive year after year, generation after generation.

The shift in power from the spiritual feminine to the egoic masculine leadership began thousands of years ago. It occurred over time as the outcome of lower-vibrational men either forcibly or through coercion took control of villages and towns. As mentioned previously, most men ruled with their ego and physical power and didn't take into consideration the effects their actions had on communities, nature, and your planet. Forests across your world were stripped and used for fuel but never replenished, leading to your current crisis in lower oxygen levels around your planet. Wars devastated entire countries and wiped out indigenous people around the world. Species of animals became extinct, and rivers and waterways polluted. It is clear to see that in the past, men allowed their egoic minds to rule instead of their balanced spirit selves. This continues to occur in many places today.

As the energy levels increase and more individuals remember who they really are, the time will be right for the world to step back and intentionally manifest their future *being* in a different way. At that tipping point on your planet, you will begin to change your government laws, processes, and goals to benefit all of humankind and your planet's ecological systems. Through the hard work and effort of many enlightened people, your planet will begin to come back into balance with all its inhabitants.

Because of the current imbalance of male/female essence, the next wave of leadership for your world will include many women. It is going to take many women to tip the scales from the current global egoic leadership to Oneness leadership creating new solutions. These new spiritually-guided leaders will bring about changes and new processes for elections and true representation of the people. People from around the world will demand changes to laws and regulations so that prejudice, greed, and corruption will no longer have a place in politics or life on your planet. Although female leaders will chart the way for the new world order for many years, your future will settle into equilibrium with balanced leadership from both men and women.

You will know your true leaders by their strong drive to work together to solve social, economic, and environmental issues and bring about the associated changes needed for equilibrium. These evolved spiritual leaders will be elected or placed into leadership positions by the enlightened many. The enlightened many will work together to bring your countries, people, and planet back into balance with what was originally intended for you. It will be of great benefit to all for everyone to work closely with these leaders and use the new energy to begin the new paradigm shift of living in Oneness.

Living in Oneness will include the need to bring everyone on your planet and nature back into balance. The shift will occur internally for each of you first. Once there is momentum of change in individuals, your local communities will naturally begin their shift at that level. As many local governments shift, states and nations will follow, and the movement will grow internationally. Showing the world how sustainability can be attained locally and then grown to a national level will allow other nations to come to know the possibility for this way of living. There is enough for everyone. Take only what you need and replenish what you take. Know that the hard work of the enlightened will eventually win out and allow peace and prosperity for all to prevail.

Women Accepting Their Power

The next step in your evolution requires women to step into their power and accept their purpose for being here. Many of you are destined to become leaders in your churches, businesses, communities, and governments. This requires you to learn and grow spiritually so that you can lead from your loving spirit self and not your egos. To become who you really are and accept your purpose for being here, you will want to spend time learning how to *be*.

There are many around you who have stepped into their power to become a beacon of light for those who are awakening. Look to these masters to assist you on your path. You are never alone in your pursuit, as many have been sent to assist you, and they will show up to you at the timing that is right for you. Listen to your spirit self to hear your daily messages. Life will flow more freely for you through this process. Encourage the enlightened women you know to step into their power to become the messengers, healers, teachers,

and leaders they are intended to be, as many are unaware of
the power they carry within their souls.

Continue to learn and understand what is occurring at this
time on your planet so that you are ready to take the next
step in your purpose. Stay grounded in God's light of truth,
and surround yourself with those who are on a similar
spiritual path. This is where you will draw your strength and
support. Many of your brothers and sister are awakening at
this time and need strong leaders such as you to guide them
on their new path. Check in with your spirit guides to hear
your guidance each morning. When the teacher is ready, the
student will appear, and when the student is ready, the teacher
will appear. There are no coincidences in the universe.

Be cautious in your approach on this path, as it is easy for
your egoic thought systems to slip back in and take charge of
your mind once again. This has been the problem throughout
your history. Don't let fear or the egoic thoughts of others
persuade you to do anything that is not in alignment with love
and what is best for all on your planet. Let love be your guide
in all that you think, do, and say. Meditate to stay connected
to the Divine Consciousness and request the assistance of the
Holy Spirit each day. When the Holy Spirit leads you in your
daily actions, you will not stray from your path or purpose.

Leadership in Advanced Societies

Leaders in advanced societies are groomed to lead. They
know their life purpose at a very early age, and their training
begins then. They are taught to incorporate the principles of
love and light in all that they do. From their inner love and
light they learn how to access their inner voice of God. From
their spirit self they call upon their guides to assist them on
their daily path. They are in constant connection with the
Universal Divine Consciousness, and each of their choices is
made from this place of this understanding. Young adults are
considered to have reached the age of reason once they have
trained themselves to access their inner voice of God at all
times and no longer have thoughts that emanate from their
egos. These are not perfect beings, and they do from time to

time have thoughts that originate from their egos. But they are easily recognized and released so that they can be replaced with thoughts that originate from their spirit self.

In advanced societies, political leaders are typically pulled from many areas in the business and public sectors where each has shown wisdom in problem resolution, sustainability, and economics. They have a history of proactively managing people and resources. Once identified, these individuals are invited to participate in political leadership mentorship programs. They learn about local, national, and international laws and their application within the respective areas they are leading. They are assigned to work with mentor leaders throughout their communities, observing and assisting with governing in that respective area. Leaders are revered and well compensated for their leadership roles. Their citizens understand the complexities of leading and appreciate their leaders for taking on these additional responsibilities, which enables their collective lives to run more smoothly. Political and business leaders are transparent in their monetary and leadership actions. Political leaders routinely publish their earnings and how they voted on each issue. They also make their banking and accounting documents available for review to anyone who requests it at any time. Their transparency allows trust to build as they continue in their leadership paths.

In advanced societies, leadership is shared amongst a group of highly-evolved spiritual leaders. No one person has control over others. Nor can one leader benefit to a higher degree from any decisions over any other person or group under their leadership. If anyone is to benefit in any way by a proposed solution, they are excused from the decision-making process so as not to influence the outcome in any way. The benefit of the ALL is the single most important factor taken into consideration in all decisions. Since they are each a part of the all, each is a benefactor of what is of the highest and best good for the all. These societies know the risks of having leaders who can be corrupted or are easily affected by negative emotions, and they are very cautious and diligent when choosing those who will lead them.

Acting counter to what is in the best interest for all beings on their planet would be a reason for a leader to be excused from any position of responsibility and decision making. Since decisions are made within a leadership group whose members have come from diverse backgrounds, potential solutions are discussed while considering as many alternatives as possible. Although it is very rare, using one's position of leadership to control or take advantage of others is also reason for dismissal from any leadership role. When a leader has failed to follow the public service code of conduct, there is a process for correction and retraining if the infraction is deemed insignificant and no one is harmed in the event. It is very rare, but if the infraction is more significant, the person is typically transferred to a position in which they are still able to pursue their purpose but do not lead others. If the infraction is illegal, then the council turns the matter over to the authorities for due process.

Business leaders are groomed in a similar fashion. Those who will eventually be responsible for a certain group of workers are trained in the specific field, such as engineering, as well as in leadership skills. They learn about the different challenges and issues that typically occur within that field and how best to resolve those issues. They learn how to cooperatively solve issues between people and how best to release egoic thoughts in those around them. They also must know problem resolution, sustainability, and economics. They need to know how to manage and allocate people and resources. If a leader wishes to change careers, they are helped to gain additional training in that field as well as the associated management challenges and resolutions for that field.

Happy people create a loving working and living environment. Making sure that all who are working in government are happy and committed in their jobs is important in advanced societies. Their wish is to keep the energy levels as high as possible in all environments and ensure that each individual enjoys what they are doing. This is a very important part of good leadership. They work diligently to ensure that each person is thoroughly appreciated and compensated for their contribution to the community.

Change Agents in Leadership

It is easy to see where change is needed once one steps back to see the corruption and greed that is so prevalent in your world today. It is not so easy to see where one would begin to tackle the process of change. The first step in bringing your governments back into balance is to ensure that you have put into place the leaders who can best govern from the universal laws. Although there may be exceptions, you cannot expect those who benefit from the current processes to want to change any part of it. Your leaders must not be allowed to receive any benefit from their position of power. Pay them well for the work they do, so that they are not tempted to act in egoic ways. Provide an equal amount of public funds for all campaigns. Set aside these funds from the taxes collected, and require candidates to account for their spending. Political candidates should be required to submit and publish detailed resumes of their education and experience in leadership, as well as their political stance in resolving the major issues facing their local communities, states, nations, and the planet. Sitting candidates should also be required to publish for all voters their complete voting history during their term of office. How can people be expected to vote for the most qualified candidates when they don't know who they are and what they stand for?

Small changes take minimal action. Complete paradigm shifts require monumental actions from all levels of your societies. Each of you must play your integral part in the shift in order for it to succeed. The role you are to play is the reason you are here now.

Chapter 15
The New Earth

Land of the Free, Home of the Brave

This chapter was added just before printing this book and is meant to cause you to reflect upon how you show up to your world today and your potential for tomorrow. I am approaching you in a writing style that is completely different from that of previous chapters. My goal is to gather your full attention so that I can engage you in a way that causes you to take action. Small changes take minimal action. Complete paradigm shifts require monumental actions from all levels of your societies. Each of you must play your integral part in the shift in order for it to succeed. The role you are to play is the reason you are here now. Many souls volunteered to be on Earth at this time, but only those here now were granted this opportunity. You were chosen because you have gifts that are needed at this time. You are each advanced souls and upon awakening, are poised to usher in the greatest period of time in Earth's history.

I invite you to step up and participate in one of the most sweeping opportunities ever made available for humans on Earth. Your planet has shifted into the fifth dimension, and you now require assistance to successfully climb the next rung of ascension spiritually. You have much to learn about many new things. These are the things that you have forgotten. To relearn these things, you must let go of the old ways. To let go of the old ways, you will need to reflect upon what is working in your life and what is not. Making the leap from the third to the fifth dimension requires you to let go of all that you thought to be true about yourselves, your history, and your presence on Earth. It requires all on your planet to undergo an internal shift in consciousness so that you can awaken to your purpose at this time. You are greatly needed, and we call to you now.

This information is meant to cause you to pause and reach back to remember 100,000 years ago in your physical incarnation history when you were living on other planets. You volunteered to descend from the higher dimensions of your home planets to go to Earth to assist in its shift to the fifth dimension. The shift is occurring now. Now is the apex of all the accumulation of time that you have been keeping the light for humanity. You have accomplished so much, and now we ask you to continue to stay focused to assist in the completion of the shift. Do you remember now? Does this resonate with you? Do you really feel this is your home? Or have you always felt like you really didn't fit in or belong? Is there something that keeps pulling at you, a knowing that there is something more out there for you? Some of you may even feel powerful emotions in reading this as you awaken to this memory at this moment.

Reflecting on Who You Are

Now that you have read this book, you have a basic understanding of what Oneness should begin to look like in your world. As with all new shifts in belief and thinking, actually incorporating change into your world may be a challenge for many of you. Without constant input and reminders, it will be easy for many to fall back into the world of egoic thoughts. We would like to ensure that this shift occurs for you in a manner that is pleasant for you. Although we can't promise you it won't be frustrating at times, Our hope is that you will embrace it with joy and see it as the gift that it truly is.

After reading all that is written here, I ask you to step back and look at how you show up in your world and your span of influence. Take a moment to visualize the interactions you have on a daily basis. How do you show up at work in each of your relationships? At home? At school? At church? At the grocery store? At the gym? At the playground? How many different hats or personas do you wear? What do these personas represent to you? Are you a different person for each area of your life? Why? Why not?

What if I could help you remember how to *be* one *being* or SELF in all areas of your life? What would that do for you? Would it simplify your life? Cause you to have less stress? Allow you the space to remember all that you are? Provide you with more time to *be* with those you love? Now ask yourself who you love. Who don't you love? Why is that? What if I could help you remember how to be LOVE to everyone you meet and show you that they can be LOVE to you? What would that do for your world? Your life? Your personal interactions each day?

What if all that you remember rocks your world in ways you couldn't possibly fathom if you lived many lifetimes? How would your world change for you? What would your world look like then? What if I could send you a personal coach, a best friend who could help you remember? What if they could teach you how to better live your life so that you could experience deep love, peace, and harmony with all beings on Earth? On other planets? Would you invite these teachers into your life? Or would you send them away? Why? Why not?

Would you be brave enough to embrace what you have forgotten if you knew that your life and your world could be a far better place to live for all people? This and much more is possible in your near future. Will you respond positively to these, your teachers, when they arrive? Or will you be fearful of them? Will you remember these wonderful beings as your ancestors, families, and friends from previous lives? Or will you believe they are here to harm you? Will you be able to forgo the fear caused by media movies and hype to greet them with great joy, knowing that your lives are about to become better in ways you thought were impossible?

Divine Plan Moving Forward

This chapter calls for you to remember the Divine plan put into place for you before you descended to Earth long ago. This plan called for your home planets to send masters,

teachers, and coaches to assist Earth in the ascension process
at this time. The many planets you left are now ready to assist
you. They are excited and joyful to finally be able to do their
part in the ascension of Earth. You have prayed for assistance,
and they are available and poised to assist you with living
your life in ways that will more quickly allow you to become
fifth-dimensional beings. They have volunteered to become
your personal, business, environmental, and governmental
masters, teachers, and coaches.

They can teach you the forgotten ways they have been
living as advanced societies for millions of years. They have
successfully traversed the levels of ascension that you are
just now being exposed to, as well as many higher. They
have assisted many other planets in their ascension process
as well. They have much to teach you about the cosmos,
parallel universes, ascension, dimensions, and universal
laws. There really is so much you do not yet remember about
your existence. Do you want to remember? Are you curious
to finally know without a doubt the answers to your many
questions of your existence within the cosmos? Are you ready
to learn more about the Divine and your divinity?

Now I ask you to pause once again and ask yourself if you
are ready to reacquaint yourselves with your families and
neighbors from your home planets without the panic and
aggression portrayed in your movies. These are your families
from the planets you left when you embarked upon your great
mission to seed Earth so long ago. These are beings of pure
love, as you are also at your core. Are you remembering?
Does this information now resonate with you? Do you now
know this is your truth?

Advanced Technologies

What if your long forgotten, family, friends and neighbors
could bring you advanced technologies? Would you embrace
them and their technologies? These technologies could
provide you with free power, advanced sciences, new
methodologies for agriculture, and communications. What if
these advanced technologies could allow you to bring your

planet back into balance with nature? What if they could teach you how to heal yourselves from diseases and maintain perfect health? Would you embrace all that could allow you to simplify your lives? Would you like to spend more time with your families and friends? Would you want to learn how to better enjoy these relationships? Would you want to live as you were always intended to? These teachers offer you this and much more.

The technologies they have to offer could free your world of hunger, illness, and poverty and allow all the beings of Earth to live their lives with all their needs met. Would you embrace these loving beings with open arms? Or would fear cause you to shrink back and run from them? Do you wish to be a student once again? This is truly the perfect example of "when the student is ready, the teacher will appear." Are you ready to be that student?

Contact with Your Governments

Now let's understand how your forgotten families and friends have tried to help Earth throughout your history. As some of you may have learned in your history classes, there have been many visits from your faraway families in Earth's history. Carvings in your ancient pyramids depict flying saucers and beings in space suits. These carvings appear in ancient sites all over your planet. Your Native Americans tell stories of being visited by beings from other stars. These visits were undertaken in an effort to help your planet remember and better understand their purpose for being here. This was done in an effort to keep the memories of your mission and Earth's ascension alive in the minds of your ancestors so that they could assist others in remembering.

The time of your awakening to your purpose and mission is upon you now. Your governments have been contacted many times in your recent past to gain permission to send teachers to assist. How would you react if you knew your governments turned down this help, saying, "Thanks, but no thanks!" Instead, they requested help in how to maintain power. Do you want these same people to speak for you now?

What would your response be if your distant families had asked you personally instead? Would you want to know more information, such as who, what, when, where and how?

What if you found out that your past families and neighbors have been helping some of your governments for more than seventy years in the hopes that your governments would finally allow them to deliver these message to you, the people of Earth, so that each of you could decide what you would like to happen for you? You have requested help, and they are the answers to your prayers. These teachers are Our means to help you learn what it is that you do not remember.

How would you approach Earth if you were the forgotten brothers and sisters coming to your planet? Would you simply show up, or would you want to be invited to visit with open arms? As good family and neighbors, they wish to be invited. Would you be willing to be one of their hosts? Would you step into the light to be a leader amongst your fellow humans? It is important that you not be fearful of these loving beings and understand their sole purpose. They have no hidden agenda and only wish to serve. They are beings of love and light and have much to teach you. You can simply request their assistance and they will be happy to help. They are merely a thought away.

Embracing Unity with Other Worlds

You are beings of free will. What will you decide for yourself? Your families? Your businesses? Your schools? Your governments? You are here on Earth because you decided to help Earth 100,000 years ago. You have been the keepers of the light for Earth during this entire time. Will you step up once again to allow the ascension to occur as planned? Reflect within your soul self and ask to know your past. Do you remember your purpose for coming here? The assistance of these enlightened beings was always a part of the master plan for the ascension of Earth. You agreed to descend with the condition that your families and friends would be willing to come back here to assist you at the time of the ascension. Now is the time for you to awaken to embrace your brothers and sisters arriving from the planets you left so long ago. They are awaiting your welcoming embrace to reunite with you once again. Do you remember? Are you ready to welcome them? The time is now upon you ...

We have asked this author to set up a website to allow you to submit your questions and have them be answered by Me, the Ascended Masters, and the Galactic Council. The Galactic Council is the leading body of the many planets from which you descended so long ago. This council is available to coordinate and assist your governments, schools, businesses, families, and individuals. Will you accept this assistance? Are you ready to host your new teachers? Please consider stepping out of your fear to embrace the love and gifts they have to offer you.

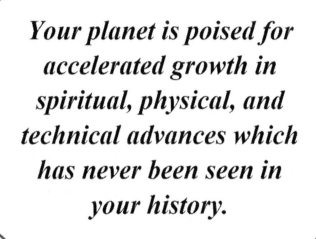

Your planet is poised for accelerated growth in spiritual, physical, and technical advances which has never been seen in your history.

Chapter 16
Your Time Has Come

Your Time Has Come

The information contained in this book is only an introduction to knowing the truth of who you are. I will provide new information in my next book about ascension, higher dimensions, sacred geometry, and other worlds. Most important, I will provide recommendations and examples of how to be in the *now* of living life. You will be sent many masters and teachers who will assist you. You have much that is provided here to begin your ascension process. Begin now, even if it is baby steps, as each step that you take leads you to the truth of who you are and the inheritance of All That Is yours.

Your time has come. You are at the threshold of a new era for the Milky Way galaxy. You have waited 100,000 years for this ascension process to begin, and the time has come. The year 2012 marked an ending to the old, and 2013 starts the beginning of the new Earth. Your planet is poised for accelerated growth in spiritual, physical, and technical advancements such as has never been seen in your history. Enjoy the process of ascension. Get excited about all the changes that will be occurring for the highest and best good of all on your planet. *Be* in the now to enjoy it fully, as this is what is intended for you.

Keep yourself in the energy of love, as that is your new way of *being*. Stay focused on your spiritual growth, and all your needs will be met as you ascend. Reach out to invite your teachers to come to you. They are excited about the possibility of assisting you, but they must be invited to participate with you. Your life is about to become much easier. You will have deeper meaning in your life. You have done it. You are at the threshold of the new Earth, and you are the change agents. Your time is now. Embrace all that the fourth, fifth, and sixth dimensions are and all that you can become within each of them.

It is indeed a beautiful event to witness. You have chosen to come to Earth at this time to experience this ascension. Many of you have experienced many events that have caused you great pain. From that pain comes great learning and spiritual advancement. You are now ready to step forward to help others awaken. The love We feel for you is immense. We are excited in our anticipation of all that can be made manifest. We honor you and all that you have accomplished. We know you will accomplish much more as you continue in your purpose and others join you.

In closing, I ask that you consider a world where love is All That Is. What would that look like for you? Take a moment and envision love fully operating in your life. Now create it, as it is yours to manifest. Watch this new life and love expand, as you cannot contain it. What beauty! What joy! This is all yours. It is your inheritance as children of God. This is the new Earth.

I send you love, blessings, and appreciation as you continue on your journey of discovery and ascension. Peace, joy, and happiness are yours.

Jesus